JOHN KNOX, well known for his books on the New Testament, is Baldwin Professor of Sacred Literature at Union Theological Seminary in New York. He has also taught at Emory and Fisk universities, the University of Chicago, and Hartford Theological Seminary.

Dr. Knox is associate editor of and contributor to *The Interpreter's Bible,* as well as author of these widely read books: *Chapters in a Life of Paul, Criticism and Faith, The Death of Christ, The Early Church and the Coming Great Church, The Fourth Gospel and Later Epistles, The Integrity of Preaching, Philemon Among the Letters of Paul,* and *Christ and the Hope of Glory.*

The Ethic of Jesus
in the
Teaching of the Church

The Ethic of Jesus
in the
Teaching of the Church

Its Authority and Its Relevance

JOHN KNOX

ABINGDON PRESS

New York • Nashville

THE ETHIC OF JESUS IN THE TEACHING OF THE CHURCH

Copyright © 1961 by Abingdon Press

Library of Congress Catalog Card Number: 61-5195

SET UP, PRINTED, AND BOUND BY THE
PARTHENON PRESS, AT NASHVILLE,
TENNESSEE, UNITED STATES OF AMERICA

To

ERNEST CADMAN
COLWELL

Long-time comrade in the search for answers to such
questions as this book considers

Foreword

The ethical teaching of the New Testament poses a serious problem for all who take it seriously; and the purpose of this book is, first, to emphasize that it must be taken seriously, and, secondly, to deal as adequately and as helpfully as possible with the resulting problem.

The first element in this purpose may seem at first gratuitous and irrelevant: Why emphasize what is so obvious? Actually, however, developments within our secular culture and within the church have combined to threaten the authority of the distinctive Christian ethic, especially as a code or principle for the ordering and disciplining of our lives as individuals. Reacting against a false legalism, we are in danger of forgetting that the Christian is subject to a more exacting ethical demand than any written code could impose—a demand from which he cannot escape and which he can disregard only at the peril of his soul. With such terms as "moralism" and "perfectionism" we have sometimes dismissed an ethical concern which belongs inalienably to the life of the Christian and have denied a personal responsibility of which we cannot rid ourselves. We are in danger of succumbing to a new antinomianism, of using such a phrase as "our freedom in Christ" to cover our selfishness and our worldliness. Now the very strenuousness of Christ's ethical demand has contributed to some extent to this result—at any rate, to the rationalizing and justifying of it—by placing the Christian under what looks like an impossible obligation. In so far as this is true, our antinomianism represents our attempt to escape from a problem which we cannot solve.

This problem, which confronts every Christian and of which every Christian is in some degree aware, can be seen perhaps most clearly from the point of view of the Christian teacher. Hence the phrase "in the teaching of the church" in the title of this book. It is important to recognize, however, that by "the Christian teacher" I am not referring to any particular vocational class. We have heard much in recent years about the distinction between teaching and preaching in the early church. The terms "kerygma" and "didache" have become virtual English words. Although it would be a mistake perhaps to suppose that any scholar has meant to propose so neat and rigid a pattern, nevertheless we have been led to envisage two distinct corps of early Christian ministers—the preachers, who proclaimed the saving event which had occurred in Christ; and the teachers, who gave instruction in the meaning and implications of the new life which the event had made possible.

8

We have good reason, I think, to be skeptical about this picture. It is striking that in none of the several accounts of the various kinds of ministry exercised in the primitive church are "preachers" mentioned. We hear of prophets and teachers, but not of preachers. Now it appears that even prophets and teachers are not to be distinguished too sharply from each other, since it seems likely that all prophets were also teachers—that is, prophets were teachers with certain ecstatic gifts or powers. But it is to be presumed that all teachers, whether prophets or not, were preachers. The proclamation of the gospel of God's action in Christ and the explication of the situation which that action had brought about were closely related, ultimately inseparable, functions; and the one could hardly have been carried on without the other.

Although the matter is, strictly speaking, not relevant to our theme, and we must spend only a moment with it, I believe it is worth pointing out that the two functions are still just as closely related to each other as they ever were and that the sharp distinction in idea and the actual separation in fact between preaching and teaching, which are often found in the modern church, are both false and baneful. The proclaimer of the good news must explain its significance—else he is proclaiming an empty thing. The explainer of the gospel's significance must also proclaim the gospel itself—otherwise the "explanation" is pointless and irrelevant. There are, to be sure, real differences between what is appropriate in the classroom and what is appropriate in the pulpit—differences in content, emphasis, and method. But if the gospel is not being proclaimed in the classroom, Christian teaching is not taking place; and if the implications of the gospel—the obligations it lays on us as well as the promises it offers us—are not being opened up in the pulpit, Christian preaching is not taking place. So that when we speak of the teaching ministry of the church we are considering, not the function of a special class, but the vocation of all who speak for Christ, whether they customarily stand in the preacher's pulpit or behind the teacher's desk, or whether they do their interpreting through writing or in other less formal ways.

I have spoken of the obligations the gospel lays on us. With the reality and nature of these obligations Christian teachers have always been in large measure preoccupied. Much of the teaching of the church has been concerned with how the Christian is obligated to live toward others and with what is the ground of his obligation. The teachers referred to by Paul as among the ministers of the early church were undoubtedly occupied in large part with formulating and promulgating what we may call the Christian ethic, as Paul himself was also. It is these teachers who are speaking in the ethical sections of all the epistles and to whom we are no doubt in debt for the blocks of Jesus' own ethical teaching which have been preserved for us. We could scarcely select a theme for discussion which would lie nearer the center of their interest and belong more essentially to a consideration of the teaching ministry

10

of the church, whether in the early period or in our own.

After some remarks, by way of reminder only, of what the distinctively Christian ethic is, we shall turn to some consideration of the problems it presents—particularly to those responsible for explaining and applying it. We shall then look at the ways in which we may seek to escape these problems—or to solve them. Finally, and at greater length, I want to deal with the way in which the ethical teaching is related to the preaching of the grace of God manifested both in forgiveness and in the new life of the Spirit.

Although these chapters were written primarily for publication, they represent substantially, with some enlargement, the Willson Lectures on Christian Education delivered in Nashville, Tennessee, in February of 1960. Some of the material had earlier been used in addresses at the United Theological Seminary and the Wesley Theological School, as well as in the C. I. Jones Memorial Lectures at the Rayne Memorial Methodist Church in New Orleans. I have also drawn freely upon some lectures given at the Butler University School of Religion and subsequently published in the *Shane Quarterly*. Permission to use this copyrighted material is gratefully acknowledged, along with the many courtesies extended to me on the various occasions I have mentioned.

JOHN KNOX

Contents

The Ethic and the Problem

If Jesus'
words, "You . . . must be perfect, as your heavenly
Father is perfect," are taken at face value, they set a
standard for our moral life which there is no possibility
of our attaining. For this reason we have often been
averse to taking them at face value, since otherwise an
intolerable logical contradiction (not to mention the
moral dilemma) would appear to be involved: how
can we be really obligated to do the impossible? One
cannot get rid of the difficulty, however, by finding
some other meaning than "perfect" for the Greek ad-
jective in this particular verse (Matt. 5:48) or by deciding that Luke's rendering "merciful" (6:36) is the
more authentic, for not only the Sermon on the Mount,
from which this text is taken, but also the teaching of
Jesus as a whole is pervaded by this conception. When
we have done all we can do, we are still unprofitable
servants. We are under a moral responsibility which

even the best effort of even the best man is utterly unable to discharge.

Perhaps the major difference between a purely rational ethic—if such an ethic be a possibility at all—and the Christian ethic lies just here. The assertion that one is morally obligated to be and do what one lacks the moral resources to be and do would appear to be absurd; but the Christian recognizes that, absurd or not, the assertion is true. As to the fact of the obligation, he knows he is subject to the law of love, to which there is no limit either intensively or extensively. Of his failure to live by it, he is equally and no less acutely aware. And not only is he aware of his present failure, he knows that so far as life in this world goes, he will never be able entirely to succeed. The Christian ethic is, in one sense at least, an impossible ethic.

In a publication of some years ago[1] I ventured to place side by side two well-known poems: one, John Drinkwater's "A Prayer," in which he has us confess that "we know the paths in which our feet should press," that God's "decrees" are written "across our hearts," but that we desperately lack the "strength to labor as we know," the "will to fashion as we feel"; the other poem, some lines of Hamlin Garland, who with equal poignancy asks for the *knowledge* of his duty. "My heart," he says, "is aflame to be right"; but he cannot see how he can be right in this complicated and tragically needy world. The poems appear to diagnose our moral problem quite differently; but actually the difference is not so great as it seems at first, for both are really testifying to the discrepancy we are now considering. Both are saying in effect, "We cannot do what we see we ought." Drinkwater finds the cause in his weakness and asks for more strength; Garland supposes he must be seeing his duty wrongly and asks for more light. Both are seeking an answer to the same problem—our apparent obligation to do what we find ourselves actually incapable of doing.

Not long ago I was speaking on this same general subject at a conference of pastors, and someone challenged my statement that no one fulfills the law of love. He knew people, the challenger said, who had done so. He mentioned as an example of this perfection the case of a woman, a devout Christian, known to many in that group and known also to many of the readers of these pages, for she is a person of some prominence. He was ready to agree that she herself would vigorously reject the ascription of goodness; but that, he felt, did not mean it was not deserved; indeed, such a denial on her part would point the other way, humility being one of the ingredients of her goodness. We could know her goodness better than she could know it herself.

There is truth in this. It might be argued that no one can know how good one is because when one is being good, one is by definition not regarding oneself at all; and if later one remembers how good one was, immediately one's goodness will seem to have turned to evil. But if it is true that only another can know how good we are, it is also true that only we ourselves

17

can know how bad we are. The full extent of the evil that is in us can never be known to another. When my friend says about himself, "There is no good in me," I am likely to protest vigorously and to say how mistaken he is. He *is* mistaken; and it is not only the part of love, it is the part of truth, to tell him so. But when he says, "There is great evil in me," I have no right to protest. To be sure, I may not be able to see the evil; but I am not in position to see it, just as he is not in position to see the good. No one who watches what goes on in his own heart is likely to be under the illusion that he obeys, or has it in his power to obey, the exalted command of Jesus. And what the psychologists can tell us and what history and the newspapers reveal give ample ground for the view that what each of us finds true of himself is true also of other men. If Jesus' ethical teaching, taken at face value, is to set the standard for our lives, we know that we have not reached, and in this life cannot reach, the point where we can say, "I have done all that is required of me."

For there can be no dispute that Jesus seems to have asked for an absolute perfection. To be sure, occasional pieces of apparently merely prudential moral teaching can be found; but these are occasional indeed, and no one would argue that they are typical. The massive, pervasive, and really characteristic ethical teaching of Jesus seems to lay on us an impossible obligation. This is the obligation of love, called in the New Testament *agape*.[2]

18

Jesus' use of the word "love" is interesting. It would seem that he employed it only in the ethical sense—that is, to designate a duty of man. He appears not to have used it in speaking of God's attitude toward us. There is only one, more than doubtful, instance of his using the noun in this connection (Luke 11:42) and no case of even the possible use of the verb. He speaks often of God as "forgiving," as showing "pity," as being "merciful"; and the conception of God as giving to the uttermost, not only of his goods but of himself, is so pervasive of the Synoptic Gospels that one can only wonder at the omission of any reference to God's "love." This is especially remarkable in view of the fact that the Old Testament speaks not infrequently of God's love and that there are many allusions to it by the rabbis. The omission becomes even more striking when it is observed how constantly Paul talks about the love of God toward us, not to speak of the later Fourth Gospel and the Johannine Epistles. Neither what lay back of Jesus nor what followed after him prepares us for the fact that he never once refers to God's love, and the silence of his teaching in this respect must be accounted one of the many fascinating mysteries of New Testament study. Whatever the explanation of this silence, it has to do, of course, only with the use of the word; as for the reality, there is no doubt that Jesus taught that we are the objects of God's love and that this love of God toward us was at the very center of his teaching.

So far as the term itself is concerned, however, it always designates in Jesus' usage God's demands on us,

19

our duty toward him and toward one another. When Jesus is asked which is the first commandment of the law, he answers (quoting Deut. 6:5): "You shall love the Lord your God with all your heart, and with all your soul, and with all your mind, and with all your strength" (Mark 12:30).

This was, of course, the answer which many a rabbi in Jesus' time also had given; and the same thing can be said of the rest of Jesus' reply. The distinction of Jesus' teaching about the requirement of love toward God lies not in its formal or conceptual character, but in the intensity and exclusiveness with which he emphasized it and in the concrete quality of the love itself as his life and words set it forth.

What does it mean that we are required to love God with our whole heart, soul, mind, and strength? It means that one is under absolute obligation to the will of God. Obedience to it is incalculably more important than food or drink or any earthly satisfaction. No other obligation can be compared with it. Even the dearest and most intimate human ties are less binding. Nothing that men or circumstances can give us can justify us in, or compensate us for, a betrayal of this supreme obligation; and nothing of which they can deprive us deserves even a second thought in comparison with the worth of loyalty to it. It is "the pearl of great price," to possess which the wise merchant will sell all that he has. We are to seek only "God's kingdom and God's righteousness." We must deny ourselves—and this means more than a mere willingness to make sacrifices on occasion, to deny things to ourselves. It means denying the self itself; it means a radical reorientation of life, the will of God rather than one's own will becoming the center. Such is the intention of Jesus' teachings about poverty of spirit, meekness, hunger and thirst after righteousness, purity of heart, and absolute freedom from cares about one's self.

Jesus follows his recitation of the Shema as the first and greatest commandment with "The second is this, 'You shall love your neighbor as yourself.'" The two belong inseparably together; love of God essentially involves attitudes toward and relationships with our fellows. The second commandment, like the first, is a commandment of the law, a quotation from Scripture, this time from Leviticus (19:18). It is fair to say, however, that although this Old Testament maxim is approved and appropriated by Jesus, one may well doubt that he quoted it with the same enthusiasm and conviction as the Shema. He had been asked about the traditional law and he naturally answered in terms of it. I doubt that the rule from Leviticus represents the way Jesus would have defined the love for neighbor which God asks of us if he had been freely choosing his own terms. A distinguished scholar writes:

Like a good Jew, he takes the sober view of the matter, and simply tells us to love our neighbors as ourselves—avoiding the fanaticism both of a vague universalism and of the impracticable idealism which says, "Thou shalt love thy neighbor more than thine own soul" (Barnabas xix, 5).[3]

21

I am not impressed by this explanation. What would the same scholar say about such sayings of Jesus as, "If any man would come after me, let him deny himself" or "If any man . . . does not hate . . . even his own life"? Is this fanaticism? Whether the answer is yes or no, can it be denied that this kind of teaching is more character-istic of Jesus than the quotation from the Leviticus code? Love of neighbor is not to be calculating and restrained, but unreserved and complete, lavish and extravagant. One must give to him who asks, regardless of the cost to oneself; far from resenting wrong suffered, one must absorb it completely and even gladly; we are to go the second mile, to give our cloak, too. We are to love our enemies as well as our friends. Many of the parables strike this same note, as when an employer pays all his laborers the same wage although some have worked only an hour, and the father rewards with a feast and with gifts an utterly unworthy son.

We are, in a word, to be perfect as God is perfect. Jesus never dilutes the righteous demands of God or adjusts them to our moral capacities. On the contrary, he presses every moral requirement to its extreme limit. The commandment against murder becomes a prohibi-tion of hatred; the commandment against adultery becomes a prohibition of lust. Jesus reveals little, if any, interest in questions of moral casuistry—that is, ques-tions of what should be done in circumstances where, as we see it, the perfect thing is too difficult, if indeed it is not, as things are, impossible. It is doubtful that Jesus would have recognized the appropriateness of the word

22

"should" in such a context. He is concerned apparently only about our ultimate obligation—our obligation to the perfect will of God. He seems to have made no effort to break down the massive weight of it into more practicable units. The requirement under which we stand is not of such kind that any man could ever conceivably discharge it—"no one is good but God alone," he says (Mark 10:18)—but we stand under it nevertheless, and no excuse is tolerable. To be sure, God is ready to forgive us freely and to the uttermost—but not to exonerate us. All possibility of self-righteous complacency or boasting is shut out. As Paul says, every mouth is "stopped." [4]

This is, of course, not the whole story, or even the more important half of it. We do not see God's requirement of us in true perspective, or even its true inner meaning, until we look also at his love for us. Indeed, if the requirement did not have its beginning and its end in his love for us, it would be a monstrous thing. To this love, with its decisive bearing upon all that has been, and will be, said about our duty, we shall be turning our attention later. At the moment, however, it is important to recognize that Jesus' ethical teaching places us under an obligation which we cannot, with our utmost effort, fully discharge.

One further question of a purely historical kind should perhaps be raised before we turn to the problems of application and of relevance with which such teaching confronts us, namely, the question of authen-

23

ticity. And here two meanings or bearings of "authenticity" may be in our minds. Perhaps the usual meaning of the question is: "Are these teachings original with Jesus? Are they genuinely and in a peculiar sense his own?" Although the question in just this form is not strictly germane to this discussion, some brief consideration of it is appropriate and may be useful. The answer to be made to it is undoubtedly Yes. It is true that the originality of Jesus' ethical teaching does not consist in the novelty of his ideas in the formal or abstract sense, as I have already had occasion to point out in a similar connection. It is not difficult to find "parallels" in the Old Testament or in later Jewish literature to most of the teachings of Jesus. To be sure, as a Jewish interpreter like Klausner is the first to acknowledge, one must search widely and through much that is uninspired if not unprofitable to find all of these "parallels." There is a concentration of exalted teaching in the Gospels which is not matched elsewhere. But when all this is said, one must recognize that Jesus' ideas were all characteristically Jewish ideas. It is an egregious mistake, for example, to suppose that Jesus invented the conception of the love of God or was the first to think of God as like a father; and such ideas as the universality of God's care and the necessity of reliance upon God's mercy rather than upon one's own merit—these, too, can be found in the Old Testament as well as elsewhere. It is equally fallacious to suppose that Jesus was the first to insist that true righteousness is a matter of the heart, and not of outward behavior only. Jesus' great originality as a teacher consists, not in the newness of his ideas taken severally and in the abstract, but in the characteristic emphases of his teaching, in the particular way in which he felt the concrete meaning, the force, of certain traditional ideas, and in the beauty and power of his speech. Others have spoken of God as Father; but no one spoke so constantly of God in this way; no one (so far as we can know) ever realized the concrete meaning of God's fatherliness in just the way Jesus realized it, and certainly no one has ever expressed that meaning so completely and so movingly. There is no true "parallel" to the parable of the Prodigal Son (Luke 15:11-32).

This same freshness of apprehension is equally in evidence at every point. That we stand under obligation to the perfect will of God was also characteristic Jewish teaching. But where do we find the real meaning of that fact so deeply felt and so powerfully expressed, and where do we find the demands of God's perfect law set forth so clearly and so boldly as in Jesus' teaching? Others have said, "You shall love your neighbor as yourself," but the parable of the Good Samaritan (Luke 10:30-37), which Jesus told to illustrate that ethical principle, bears the unmistakable hallmark of Jesus. Jesus understood the concrete meaning of the formal requirement in a way quite uniquely his own: the fact that it was a Samaritan who showed mercy on a Jew, although Jesus and his audience were Jews, and the utter lavishness of this stranger's compassion. In the same way, the prohibition of revenge is common teaching, but it was Jesus who said: "If any one strikes you on the right cheek, turn to him the other also; and if any one would sue you and take your coat, let him have your cloak as well; and if any one forces you to go one mile, go with him two miles. Give to him who begs from you, and do not refuse him who would borrow from you" (Matt. 5:39-42). Others had warned against overweening anxiety, but Jesus' words about the fowls of the air and the lilies of the field are his very own. There is a radical character about many of the teachings of Jesus and a bold imaginative quality which place them altogether in a class apart. They convey not only a man's ideas, but the profound and the profoundly moving meaning those ideas had for the man himself. The words of Jesus are, in a sense entirely unique, living words. They can hardly be distinguished from his actions. They are in the deepest sense authentic words of Jesus.[5]

But the word "authentic" has another bearing. Are the characteristic ethical teachings of Jesus also authentically Christian? Were they accepted as normative by the primitive church, and was this acceptance of them an essential element in its nature? Do they belong fully and indigenously to the Christian life? Do they tell us something, not only about the character and genius of Jesus, but also about the Spirit which animated the early community? The fact that the teachings belong to the most primitive traditions of the church is itself evidence that they do. These strange commands of Jesus were remembered and preserved, not primarily because of interest in, admiration for, or even loyalty to, a great individual of the past, but because that same individual,

Note

26

giving the same kind of commands, was realized as present within its own existence. It is not simply Jesus of Nazareth, but also the Lord of the church, who is speaking in the Gospels. But not in the Gospels only—additional evidence of this identity can be found in the epistles. Does not the same ethical teaching as appears in the Sermon on the Mount appear in the twelfth chapter of Romans, the thirteenth chapter of I Corinthians, the third chapter of I Peter, not to speak of innumerable scattered passages? We are not confusing disciples with Master. There can be no doubt in whose words the characteristic teaching first appeared. The Master's words have a freshness and a power we shall not find in those of his disciples, and there are plenty of indications of the church's inability always to maintain the ethic in its full height and purity, of its yielding to the temptation to moderate and temper its strenuous demands. Still, taken as a whole, the epistles bring us the same high ethic as the Gospels and place us under the same limitless obligation of the love which "bears . . . believes . . . hopes . . . endures all things" (I Cor. 13:7), which does not return "evil for evil or reviling for reviling" (I Pet. 3:9), which "binds everything together in perfect harmony" (Col. 3:14), which does not take thought for the things of itself but only and always for the things of others (Phil. 2:4).

Such love, I repeat yet again, asks for more than we can give and places us under an obligation we cannot discharge. I do not need to argue that this is true or at-

tempt any precise or extended analysis of the grounds
of our inability to rise to the full demands of love. Both
the fact and the major grounds of it are apparent—
only too painfully apparent to each of us. Except possibly for occasional brief moments of superhuman insight and heroism, perfect disinterestedness and the complete denial of self are beyond the capacity of our human
nature. We are as natural finite men self-centered—this
is neither wrong nor avoidable; it is our nature—but as
sinful men we are also, equally inescapably, corrupted
by pride. Our self-centeredness passes inevitably into
selfishness. These limitations belonging to our nature
coincide with, and are inextricably involved with, the
limitations imposed by the structures of society, into
which the selfishness of other generations of men has
been built and from the evil operations of which no
man can hold aloof. We can recognize, in penitence, that
we could be more loving, more devoted to the common
good than we are; but we cannot, in truth, acknowledge
that it lies even within our power fully to obey the law
of Christ.

Such a situation, as we have seen, manifestly confronts
us with a perplexing logical problem (how can we be
really obligated to do what we cannot do?) and also with
a much more poignant personal existential problem
(how can I actually live in so impossible a position?).
These problems, and especially the latter, will never
be far from the center of our attention in this discussion. But the ethic we are considering is bound also to

Kant — We as rational creatures obey no law we do not give

He & others believe that if they are unable to perform the task they are freed from the obligation to do it

raise in our minds certain more objective and prag-
matic questions, which are particularly relevant to the
teacher's task. Two of these are especially important:
First, is so exalted an ethic able to give the direction
and support actually needed by individuals and so-
cieties? And, secondly, may such an ethic not be actually harmful in discouraging ethical activity and
impairing the ethical will? Much in this book will be
concerned, in one way or another, with possible answers to these questions. Just now we are seeking to see
as clearly as possible the meaning of the questions
themselves.

ethic = rule or law?

NO!

First, then, must we not recognize the plausibility
of the contention that the New Testament ethic does
not give us the practical guidance we often desperately
need in our ethical dilemmas? Does it help us to be told
the perfect thing to do, when we are not in position to
do the perfect thing, whether because the external situation does not allow of its being done or because we ourselves are morally incapable of doing it? We are told
(Luke 12:13-21) that on one occasion a man whose
brother apparently had stolen his inheritance came to
Jesus with his problem. Jesus refused even to discuss it,
but instead said to the complainant in effect, "Renounce
covetousness, and you won't care whether you get your
inheritance or not; indeed, you will be glad to let your
brother keep it." But actually the man was unable to
renounce covetousness; besides, he probably felt that a
matter of justice and equity was involved. To this particular man in his particular situation, it may be held,

it wasn't meant to the guidance is to come from relationship to the Holy Spirit

Don't these demands placed upon us derive from the encounter with the Risen Christ — therefore do we not only receive the demand and the grace sufficient to enable us to meet the demand for obedience

29

Jesus said nothing really useful. Nor, it is further contended, does he (or the New Testament) still have anything really useful to say to those who come with questions as to what one should do in situations where the perfect thing, for one reason or another, cannot be done.

But if this inadequacy is felt in the sphere of the ethics of individuals in their relations with one another, it is even more likely to appear in the field of what we have come to call social ethics. The late Arthur E. Holt once wrote:

> For a long time it has seemed to [me] that New Testament ethics lack some of the firm, realistic content of Old Testament teaching. They lack the sense of community which is ever present in the Old Testament. The Old Testament writers were trying to build a community. The New Testament writers seem to be dealing with abstractions.[6]

Who can fail to feel the force of Dr. Holt's contention? The Old Testament ethic *is* a social ethic in a sense and degree in which the New Testament ethic seems not to be. The Christian teacher concerned to present the demands of social justice will probably find himself drawing more upon the Old Testament than upon the New. I feel sure Dr. Holt was wrong in suggesting that the New Testament writers lacked a sense of community. I should say that the sense of community is quite as strong in the New Testament as in the Old—perhaps stronger. The difference lies rather in the fact that the religious community to which the prophets spoke was also a self-contained social, economic, and political community, whereas the early Christian community was made up of scattered groups without political power and with no sense of responsibility for the organization of society. But however the defect is explained, the New Testament, it can be plausibly contended, does not give the help we need in dealing with the large-scale social ethical problems which confront us.

A second question which challenges the teacher of the New Testament ethic is whether such teaching may not do more harm than good, having the effect of discouraging ethical action and weakening the ethical will. This is true, it may be argued, because emphasis upon an impossible perfection destroys incentive for trying to be as good as it is possible for one to be. One is in danger of doing nothing just because one cannot do all that is asked. Montefiore, the able and sympathetic Jewish student of the Gospels, voices the complaint of many that Jesus' ethical teaching is "strung too high," that it fails to have results even as good as less imaginative and less ambitious codes manage to produce. The Jewish ethic, it is acknowledged, may be less pure and strenuous; but it has the virtue of not demanding more than human nature can give. You may require that another not take vengeance on his enemy, with some hope that he will obey your injunction; but if you go beyond this and ask him to love his enemy, you ask the impossible. "Hence your command is neglected and the result of this unpractical injunction is that things are worse than they were. The bow is so bent that it snaps altogether." [7] Klausner also writes in this same vein.[8] We do not need to share all the presuppositions of these Jewish scholars in order to recognize the peril of one's doing nothing because one can only despair of doing all one should.

Closely related to this is the danger, implicit in any high idealism, of supposing that one can be good, as it were, vicariously; that one can "take out" one's goodness by thinking about it; that contemplating the good is the same thing as being good; that we are less selfish because we admire unselfishness; that we are less proud because we admire humility. It is easily possible to suppose that to think on these good things is really to possess them, or perhaps better, that thinking on them relieves us of all obligation to possess them. In the same way one may feel that to confess one is selfish is as good as being unselfish and that to admit one is proud or lustful is as good as being poor in spirit or chaste; that one achieves virtue by paying tribute to virtue and acknowledging one's lack of it.

Edwin Rogers Embree published an article some years ago with the thesis, "Religions Go by Contraries." [9] The essay purported to be an account of a conversation in Peking between a Chinese philosopher and a varied assortment of Occidentals and others. The philosopher's point was that a man's religion does not represent what he is, but what he is not; and that the lower one's attainments as regards some particular virtue, the higher one's religion is likely to be in that same respect to atone for one's failure or lack. He illustrated his point by showing that Christianity with its emphasis upon meekness, nonaggressiveness, and improvidence has been adopted largely by just those peoples in the world that are least meek, most aggressive, and most given to careful planning for the morrow; while Mohammedanism with its insistence upon care and discipline, cleanliness, punctuality, system and order, self-respect, and self-assertion has spread chiefly among peoples who are least self-assertive, least provident, least concerned about cleanliness and order. There were other illustrations of what, if it is not truth, is half-truth; and the essay in any case reminds us of the danger to which so exalted a norm as the Christian ethic makes us liable, the danger of becoming like the hypocrites who imagine that they are better than other men simply because they talk about more exalted virtues.

So much by way of a quick look at the New Testament ethic and some of the problems which it poses for those responsible for promulgating and applying it, not to speak of the more poignant personal problem with which it confronts those, teachers and others, who seek to live by it. It goes without saying that we cannot rest self-assured and complacent in so problematical a situation, and it is not strange that we should try to extricate ourselves from it by simply denying in various ways that Jesus meant to place us under so exalted and exacting a demand. In the next two chapters we shall look first at these ways of escape from the problem and then at more realistic ways of dealing with it.

Ways of Escape

In the preceding chapter we were considering the highly distinctive character of Jesus' ethical teaching. We reminded ourselves that it asks of us nothing short of perfection. We are to be devoted entirely and without reservation of any kind to the will of God, and this will for us is a complete denial of self and a love for others which knows no limit in either its depth or its range. We saw also that this way of understanding our duty, although it bears the unmistakable signature of Jesus and the marks of his own peculiar genius, was formative of the Christian community and deeply characteristic of its life, so that for us to belong to the church is to find ourselves answerable to the ethical demands of the Gospels. But here, as we saw, a serious difficulty arises: these demands are quite beyond our power to fulfill. This contradiction confronts us with problems—theoretical, personal, and practical. How can we make tolerable, and make tolerable sense of, such a situation, whether for ourselves or for others?

It is not surprising that we should first seek an escape from our dilemma by asking whether, after all, we can have truly understood the Christian ethic. The "absolute" quality in Jesus' ethical teaching as it stands—even after critical examination, indeed particularly then—can hardly be questioned; but many have wondered whether he really meant his words seriously and literally. I shall mention briefly the several forms this question takes and then proceed, at somewhat greater length, to answer them.

He is God!

Some would emphasize that Jesus was an Oriental teacher and, moreover, an Oriental teacher with extraordinary gifts of imagination and poetic speech. Extravagant metaphor and simile, lavish hyperbole would come naturally, inevitably, to his lips and would not have been misunderstood by his first hearers. What he meant was something much more moderate, more "reasonable," than his words, taken with bare literalness, would convey. Others seek escape from the difficulty by pointing out that Jesus in his ethical teaching was not laying down "rules" to be strictly followed, but rather "great principles" to which his hearers were expected to give a kind of general approval, without commitment as to the application of the principles to actual situations. A very similar point is made by those who argue that Jesus' ethical teachings do not so much lay on us obligations or demands as hold up ideals toward which we are expected to strive. There is, to be sure, an obligation to move in their direction, but not to attain them. Others again would hold that in his more strenuous teachings

35

Jesus was addressing his own disciples as a special vocational class. He did not mean that everyone should deny one's self and love one's enemies, should give to every borrower and renounce all earthly cares; these are counsels of perfection which only a very few persons could hope to fulfill, and even then only if they were freed from certain normal responsibilities and maintained in that position of freedom by the great majority not subject to so high a code.

Yet others seek escape from the dilemma through what is alleged to be the true understanding of the word "love" in the New Testament. This argument can be understood only against the background of some linguistic facts. The term for "love" in the Greek New Testament is normally *agape* (verb: *agapan*), but nothing we know about the common meaning of this term throws much light upon its significance there. Indeed, the reverse is true: it is the character of the love which the New Testament sets forth (most often without using the word) which determines the meaning of the term. In the period there were three important Greek words for love—*eran, philein,* and *agapan.* The first of these (*eran*) means passionate desire (not necessarily sensual) for another person; and *philein,* liking another person or caring for him, "loving" in the ordinary, nonerotic sense. *Agapan* is less definite in meaning and is of unknown etymological origin. It carries, we are told,

none of the magic power of Ἔρως [*eros*] and hardly any of the warmth of φιλία [*philia*] . . . . Its meaning is colourless

36

and indefinite . . . . Quite frequently it is a mere synonym, being added to the other verb for the sake of impressiveness, or substituted for it as a stylistic variant.[10]

It was apparently the Septuagint which was first responsible for giving the word (noun and verb) greater definiteness and depth of meaning and for making it readily available to the New Testament writers and their community. The word for "love" in the Hebrew Old Testament is *'ahebh,* which, somewhat like our English term, carries a wide range of meanings. It can "mean overwhelming passion that unites husband and wife (Song viii, 6 f.) , the unselfish loyalty of friends (I Sam. xx) , or resolute devotion to righteousness (Ps. xlv, 7) ." It is a strong rich term, concrete and definite to the point of exclusiveness: "The love which is commended in the Old Testament is the jealous love which chooses one object among thousands and holds it fast with all the strength of its passion and its will, brooking no relaxation of the bond of loyalty." [11] The translators of the Old Testament into Greek decided upon *agape* (and *agapan*) , not because it conveyed the robust and passionate meaning of the Hebrew term, but apparently because it was less limited to other different and lesser meanings (than the other available words) , as well as because it was a

suitable vehicle for the ideas of choice, special attention and willingness to help, which are integral to the Old Testament understanding of love. But the real victor in this competition is the old Hebrew, *'ahebh,* which enriched the vague

37

Greek word with the full strength of its meaning. It used to be thought that ἀγάπη [agape] was a new word coined by the Septuagint, but this view is no longer considered probable. What is much more important is the fact that the Greek translation of the O. T. has given new values to the whole ἀγαπᾶν [agapan] family of words.[12]

So much for the background history of *agape*.

Seizing on the fact that the term used in the New Testament is not *philia* or *eros,* modern interpreters emphasize the moral element in *agape* and argue that it is subject to the will in a way in which love often is not. Even Montefiore, a Jewish interpreter with no apologetic incentive, can make this point, although he does not regard it as really solving the problem. Speaking of love for enemies as Jesus commanded it, he writes: "What does 'love' mean? It means 'Desire their well being'; 'Do good to them'; 'Pray for their salvation.' It does not mean: 'Feel for them an emotion such as you feel for your wife, your sister or your father.' *Agapan* is not *philein*." [13]

C. H. Dodd writes in a similar vein:

Provisionally we might say that *agape* is energetic and beneficent good will which stops at nothing to secure the good of the beloved object. It is not primarily an emotion or an affection; it is primarily an active determination of will. That is why it can be commanded, as feelings cannot.[14]

And that is why, it is argued, the ethical demands of Je-

38

sus are not so clearly and starkly impossible as they appear at first to be.

Finally, refuge can be taken in eschatology: in his most characteristic ethical teaching, it is argued, Jesus was being consciously affected by his vivid expectation of the end of the age. This claim is used in two ways. Some interpreters urge that Jesus in giving his ethical teaching was thinking only of the brief interim before the Kingdom should arrive. In that interim one should live as he commanded—and indeed one might do so, since the powers of the imminent Kingdom were already breaking in and one could do what, under normal conditions, would be impossible. His ethic was an interim ethic and was not intended for the long centuries history was to last. Others use the idea of the interim in another way, but with the same effect. Jesus, they say, did not mean that his hearers were actually subject to the exalted norms his teachings seemed to set up. These norms were not suited to the conditions of this world at all and were not conceived of as embodying the obligations of men in history. But history was soon to end; the kingdom of God was already coming within sight. Jesus is preoccupied with the vision of it and of the new life we shall enjoy within it. He therefore disregards the interim entirely and devotes himself to describing the ethical spirit which will pervade the new order so soon to be established.

What are we to say about these efforts to make Jesus' ethical teachings practical? In general, we must say, I think, that they do not succeed, although some truth must be acknowledged in each of the several claims. As for the first of them, it is true that Jesus' teaching is full of extravagant images which it would be absurd to take literally. But the issue we are discussing is concerned with something more substantial than these images, however characteristic and important and however integral to his teaching they may be. When Jesus speaks of persons with beams in their eyes trying to get specks out of the eyes of others, no one will suppose that he intends anyone to take him literally. But the real question has to do with the substance of his statement, his absolute prohibition of censoriousness: "Judge not, that you be not judged." Did he mean this absolutely or not? When he was asked, "How often shall my brother sin against me, and I forgive him? As many as seven times?" was Jesus exaggerating when he answered, "Seventy times seven"? When questions like this are asked about the substance of Jesus' teaching, I can see only one answer as possible. He did mean what he said. To conclude that Jesus did not mean his "absolutes" absolutely would involve ascribing to him a lack of responsibility and seriousness which no student of his teaching and life as a whole would find credible.

As to the distinction between "rules" and "principles," one may acknowledge it without feeling that it solves our problem. "Principles," as I understand the term in this connection, differ from "rules" in two respects: they are more general and inclusive, and they are more concerned than "rules" are with inner spirit or intention.

But are "principles" any less mandatory? Are not "principles" as well as "rules" concerned with obligation? ↙ If so (and I do not see how we can answer that question otherwise), not only do we not solve the problem created by the "hardness" of Jesus' ethical teaching by this emphasis upon "principles," but we render it more difficult. We sometimes talk as though a "principle" were easier than a "rule"; but can it be easier to obey a very general command applying to the whole area of our experience and touching our inner thoughts and motives as well as our conduct than to obey a very specific regulation? Is it not obviously ever so much harder? It is undoubtedly true that Jesus was concerned with principles in the sense in which we have defined the term. When he says, "If any one strikes you on the right cheek, turn to him the other also," he is not laying down a rule to be strictly and exactly followed. It would be quite absurd to suppose that he was. But what *was* he doing? Was he not saying that when we are wronged, not only must we not retaliate, but we must not even resent the injury; that we must respond with active good will, overcoming evil with good? And is not this infinitely more difficult than the observing of any mere rule could be?

But, as we have seen, some insist that Jesus did not mean that we should actually put any such principles into effect. These principles were only "ideals," which we should try to keep before our eyes and toward which we should try to move as rapidly as the conditions of our existence permit; they were not intended to present

41

God's actual demands on us. Now there can be no doubt that the higher and more strenuous teachings of Jesus do indeed actually function for us in some such way. But the question is whether Jesus so intended them; and this question, I think, must be answered in the negative. To attribute such an intention to him would be to make him consciously the romantic visionary he has sometimes been interpreted as being. Can we really read Jesus' greatest teachings—that is, read them with careful attention—and for a moment suppose that he was not stating with terrible earnestness (notwithstanding the charm, and even humor, of his speech so often) what he knew to be the will of God? These greatest words of Jesus are, in intention, not adumbrations of human ideals, but statements of God's awful demands. Their mood and tone authenticate them as such, as well as all we know of Jesus' life and teaching as a whole. He was intending to confront us with the will of God, which demands our whole allegiance without reservation, however prudent or logical.

The fourth claim—that Jesus' most characteristic ethical teachings were intended to apply only to a special class—must also be rejected, although again some basis for it can be allowed. It is not unlikely that Jesus laid special obligations upon those who accepted his call to become his disciples, in the sense of actually accompanying him on his journeys and sharing his life. Such persons, for example, were required to leave their families; it is unlikely that Jesus asked all his hearers to make a similar renunciation. It is possible also that the

requirement of absolute poverty should be understood
as having the same limited application, although here
one must be more cautious. But in instances like this
we are dealing with what might truly be called "rules"
and therefore with only a small part of Jesus' ethical
teaching. It is incredible that the great ethical principles
with which his teaching is so largely concerned were
thought of otherwise than as universally binding. They
are presented in the context of human life itself, not in
the context of the experience of any limited vocational
group. We are to do good to one another because God
gives his rain and sun to us all. We are to live without
care because the birds and flowers do: "If God so clothes
the grass of the field . . . will he not much more clothe
you?" One cannot believe that in such a context he was
thinking, not of human beings as such, but of some
special group of them. Moreover, to suppose that Jesus'
ethical teaching was concerned with the behavior of
only a small group of men is to rob it of seriousness and
importance almost as decisively as when others reduce
it to mere rhetoric; and the supposition becomes, therefore, in the light of Jesus' whole life and teaching,
equally impossible.

And what can be said about the argument based upon
the meaning of *agapan*—the argument that the particular kind of "love" asked of us is subject to the will as
other kinds of love, which largely involve the feelings,
cannot be? Common and attractive as this explanation
is, I should say that it only partly explains, if even that
much can be said for it. Certainly "energetic and bene-

43

ficent good will which stops at nothing" (Dodd's definition of *agape*) would seem to imply a good deal as
to what are generally called "the feelings." Paul seems
to say as much when he writes (in I Cor. 13:3), "If I
give away all I have, and if I deliver my body to be
burned, but have not love [*agape*], I gain nothing."
The difference between *philia* and *agape* in this connection would seem to lie, not in the fact that one involves feeling or emotion and the other does not, but
rather in the nature of the feeling or emotion in each
case. Undoubtedly the "love" God requires of us is
agape. Philia is ethically irrelevant or at least compara-
tively so. If, when Dodd speaks of *agape* (and not *philia*)
as being "commanded," he means "required" or "demanded," his statement is clearly true. But if the word
"command" implies the possibility of obedience—that
is, if to say that love can be "commanded" means that
it can at our will be called up or summoned—then it
is by no means clear that the distinction between *agape*
and *philia* is really pertinent. Montefiore has pointed
out that *agapan* is not *philein;* but neither is it *agatho-
poiein* (to do good) —as though it were a matter of deeds
only. The very passage in Matthew on which Montefiore
is commenting (Matt. 5:21 ff.) clearly distinguishes between outer behavior and inner attitude and insists that
it is precisely a certain inner attitude which God requires. Perhaps there does not need to be a "tender
emotion" toward our neighbors, but it is demanded that
we "*desire* their well being," that we "have good *will*
toward them"; and the problem remains of how such an

44

attitude can be either appropriately commanded or obediently given.

We come finally to the most formidable objection to the argument that Jesus was setting forth in his ethical teaching his understanding of God's will for man everywhere and at any time—namely, the claim that his teaching was consciously conditioned by his eschatology, his expectation of the early end of this age. That Jesus did in fact entertain such an expectation can scarcely be doubted except by those who are prepared to discount in the most drastic fashion the accuracy of the gospel reports of his teaching; and that his eschatology must be thought of as having a bearing of some sort on his ethics has also long been recognized and must be acknowledged. But what exactly is that bearing? In just what way does Jesus' expectation of the early end of this world and the coming of the kingdom of God need to be taken into account by the student of his ethical teaching? I have mentioned two possible answers to that question: (1) He was intending his ethical teaching only for the brief interim before the kingdom of God should come; and (2) his ethic was the ethic of the Kingdom itself and was not intended to apply until after the brief interim had passed. What are we to say of these attempts to solve the problem created by Jesus' apparently unpractical ethical teaching by making use, in these quite opposite ways, of the idea of the "interim"?

As to the first of them—the claim that Jesus was thinking only of the interim—I believe that we must recognize the plausibility of the argument and the very

45

limited and partial truth in it. The argument is that Jesus made such strenuous and uncompromising demands because he knew they could be fulfilled in the period of history which still remained—a period so short that the acceptance of so radical a world-denying ethic was practicable, and a period so great, so filled with mighty hopes, that such self-denial, even on the part of ordinary men, was possible. He was not thinking of a continuing history, an indefinitely extended future time. This last statement must surely be accepted: he was not thinking of us or of the centuries which separate our time from his. The question, however, is whether his ethical teaching would have been less absolute in its demands if he had been. To answer a question about what might have been is always precarious; but I should say that the teaching would not have been essentially different. Perhaps in that event he would have said some things he did not say; I do not believe he would have withheld anything he did say. For Jesus is concerned in his ethical teaching with the absolute will of God and would have declared it in similar terms in any case.

As to the second view—namely, that Jesus, far from being preoccupied with the interim, disregarded it entirely, giving us in his ethical teaching a description of the way of life which would belong to the Kingdom when it should come but which, he well knew, could not be normative for life in the present world—this can be rejected much more readily and summarily. To be sure, Jesus gives us in his teaching the ethic of the king-

46

dom of God. Who can doubt that this is true? His ethical teaching belongs too integrally with his teaching about the Kingdom for any other conclusion to be possible. But to agree so far does not mean agreement that this solves our problem. For one must still ask how the kingdom of God is related to man's present life. Is the Kingdom purely future, so that the ethic of the Kingdom has a merely future relevance? If this is true, the problem disappears. Jesus did not mean that we are now under obligation to a law which we cannot obey. That law will not become valid and operative until the conditions of a new and divine order make obedience not only possible but also easy and, indeed, inevitable. But, again, does not such an understanding deny to Jesus' ethical teaching the integrity and seriousness which it so manifestly possessed? Besides, it is impossible to do justice to Jesus' teaching about the Kingdom without recognizing that the Kingdom cannot be identified simply and only with a future order. God does not stand aloof from history, merely waiting to intervene when the time comes for bringing it to an end. He was the God of history and his perfect law was the true law of history: "Thy will be done on earth as it is done in Heaven."

No reference has thus far been made to what is perhaps the most distinctively contemporary way of turning the edge, so to speak, of Jesus' ethical teaching. Mention at least should be made of it here, although much in the rest of this book will be concerned more or less explicitly with the critical consideration of it. I am speaking of the tendency to weaken, if not destroy, the imperative force of Jesus' teaching through a certain way of understanding and emphasizing the *grace* of God and the freedom it confers. A reaction against legalism issues in a virtual antinomianism. But, whatever may be said about the logic of this reaction, it is hard to interpret the Gospels in so radical a way. In so far as New Testament texts can be cited in support of so wholesale a rejection of law, they are to be found in Paul's rather than in Jesus' teaching; and either Paul's supposed position is tacitly or frankly preferred by proponents of such views, or else, by the most violent methods of exegesis, Jesus' teaching is brought into line with what are taken to be Paul's ideas. With the question of what Paul's position was in this regard, as well as with the whole problem of the bearing of God's grace upon his ethical demands, we shall be dealing in the final two chapters of this book.

More needs to be said just here, however, about a less extreme manifestation of this same tendency. This is the assertion that no general statement as to the nature and content of God's will for us is possible. To be sure, God does make absolute ethical demands on us, but he makes these demands directly, immediately, individually, and always within the context of actual life situations. There is no universal or generally binding "law" of God, and it is a mistake to suppose that Jesus thought so. God tells each of us what he is to do in his own situation. General ethical teaching can be suggestive or illustrative, but not normative. With this position we

48

can agree to the extent of acknowledging that there is no "law of God" if by that phrase we mean some code or legal instrument standing between God and us. God's relations with us are immediate and personal, and his will for us is a personal will. We are to obey *him*, not his "law." But if what he asks of me he asks also of others, and if what he asks is in conformity with his nature so that he cannot but ask it, I see no objection to speaking of the *law* of God or the *law* of love.

In a significant book on the structure of the New Testament ethic, Joseph Sittler writes:

These teachings of Jesus are not the legislation of love (the very term contradicts the nature of love) but are rather the paradigms of love. System is proper to the inorganic; the living has a characteristic *style*. Jesus in his teaching did not attempt a systematization or exhaustive coverage of all areas of human behavior. He did not, after the manner proper to philosophers of the good, attempt to articulate general principles which, once stated, have then only to be beaten out in corollaries applicable to the variety of human life. He speaks, rather, of God and of man and of the human community in a relational and a living fashion, and on the way, in the course of his speech swoops down, now here, now there; picks up some detail, situation, instance of human pathos, error, pride, holds it up for a moment, and then moves on.[15]

With this I can fully agree, provided it is recognized that the "style" is a consistent one and provided also it is understood that the teachings, while nonlegislative

49

in the sense of not laying down adequately comprehensive rules, or indeed rules at all, are nevertheless concerned with the question, "What are we required to be and do?" and that they give a coherent answer to that question. These provisions are, from my point of view, very important.

From all of this it may be concluded that we cannot resolve the apparent contradiction of our ethical position as Christians, standing as we do under a requirement which we cannot fulfill—we cannot solve our problem by reinterpreting the ethical teaching of Jesus. Perhaps the strongest argument against the truth of any such "solution" is the fact that the early church, which stood nearest to the teaching and presumably remembered it most vividly, did not understand its intention in any of the several ways we have been considering in this chapter. As we have seen, the ethical sections in the New Testament epistles faithfully echo the Gospel words. The primitive Christians understood Jesus to have meant what he said. And so must we. There is no way of denying his intention to place us under the exalted and exacting demand which his most characteristic teachings so clearly embody.

But even if there were a way of denying this, our problem would remain. It has a deeper, more existential ground than the reported sayings of Jesus and the exhortations of the apostles. We are not in the position of having to wait upon an interpretation of some ancient words to know what kind of obligation we are under.

I do actually find myself under an impossible demand. I know I am deceiving myself when I set any limits to my ultimate moral obligation. I know I am deluding myself when I imagine I have reached, or can reach, the point where I can say: "I have done all I ought to do. I am all I ought to be." Thus, if Jesus had not, in his most characteristic teaching, defined God's will for us in terms of utterly unqualified and unrestricted good will, one can reverently say, "He should have." Nothing short of that would have been true to what, at our deepest and best, we know to be true about God and about ourselves. We would not have known this about God and about ourselves if Jesus had not made it known. But once he has made it known, we see for ourselves that it is true: that is, it finds us at our deepest and most real.

All creative insight, whatever its ultimate source, has this kind of existential validation. Revelation does not so much give us new truth as make us aware of truth which, it seems, we once knew but had forgotten, just as redemption is not so much the creation of the new as it is the restoration of the old. To be saved is not to be someone else, but one's own true, "original" self. The law of love, which is the law of Christ, is no superimposed command that we may accept or reject, depending upon how we decide either the historical question about the intention of Jesus or the practical question of how the law of love would actually work out. That law is the law of our own life. It is the voice of the eternity in our heart. It is part of the evidence, present in our being, that man essentially and ultimately belongs, not

51

to this world and age, but to the kingdom of God; and that he is subject to a demand higher and more exacting than any human tribunal can impose, any human wisdom can justify, or any human effort can fulfill.

This is our situation, regardless of what we may find it possible or plausible to do with the teaching of Jesus or any other code. The problem would appear to be both inescapable and insoluble. What, then, can we do to be saved? What is the answer, if not to the theoretical question, at least to the practical and existential dilemma? In particular, what is the task and opportunity of the Christian teacher?

III

Approaches to Solution

We have twice recalled Jesus' words summing up an impressive section of the Sermon on the Mount: "You . . . must be perfect, as your heavenly Father is perfect." It is striking and at first sight seems strange that one who conceived of human obligation in such exalted terms should have been called the friend of sinners. And yet it is thus that he was widely, and perhaps most characteristically, known. The familiar series of parables in the fifteenth chapter of Luke, the parables of the lost sheep, the lost coin, and the lost son, is presented as an answer to opponents who made this assertion as a charge against him. Jesus did not deny the charge; rather, he said in effect what on another similar occasion (Mark 2:17) he said in so many words: "I came not to call the righteous, but sinners." If this had not been true, of course, he would not have come to call us, or any other human being, and you and I could have no part with him. And in so far as we succeed in convincing our-

53

selves, as sometimes in our pride we try to do, that we are good people, we separate ourselves from Christ. As a matter of fact, however, we do not succeed in doing this, or at any rate we do not succeed for long. As we have been reminding ourselves, if we are sensitive and alive at all or halfway honest, the recognition is forced on us that we are under obligation, not to our own reasonable and comfortable standards, or to society's reasonable and comfortable standards for us, but to God's requirement of disinterested love, to which there is no limit either in depth or range. We know, at least in such moments of insight, that we have not reached—and moreover that in this life we never shall—the point where we can say: "I have done all I ought to do; I am all I ought to be."

I've done my Best

This means, of course, that any true peace we have—that is, any peace which is soundly based and permanent and not a mere callous complacency—must rest, not upon our either ignoring or eliminating the evil in ourselves, but upon our recognizing the good in others, especially in One Other; or, to say the same thing differently, such peace must consist, not in the awareness of being worthy, but in the assurance of being accepted in spite of our unworthiness, not in the consciousness of being good enough to be loved, but in the knowledge that Another is good enough to love us; or, to use more traditional theological language, it must rest, not upon our works, but upon God's grace.

forgiveness & love of God

Here, in the forgiveness and love of God, lies the ultimate answer to the problem we have been discussing;

54

and the meaning of it—particularly certain aspects of that meaning—will be under consideration in the final two chapters of this book. Meantime, however, something further needs to be said about the New Testament ethic itself and the problem its absoluteness creates for those who must make immediate moral decisions, and particularly for those who are responsible for giving moral guidance to men and nations—a problem which the recognition of our ultimate dependence upon grace alone by no means entirely removes.

We have often alluded to our inability to obey what the gospel commands as being an obvious fact, and thus far have made no effort to analyze the grounds of our failure, although reference was made at one point to our finiteness, our sinful selfishness and pride, and our inescapable involvement in a finite and sinful society. Even now nothing in the way of formal or systematic analysis will be attempted; but we may be helped to see the problem of this chapter more clearly if we give attention to some one of Jesus' characteristic teachings and the difficulties it involves for us if we take it seriously.

Let us consider, as our example, the familiar injunction in Matt. 5:42: "Give to him who begs from you, and do not refuse him who would borrow from you." We may begin by acknowledging with those who would minimize the rigor of this command that this is not a rule to be obeyed in literal, mechanical fashion. What someone asks in any particular case may not be what he

really needs, or even most wants (like the lame man at
the gate of the temple in Acts 3:2-10) ; or it may be that
we simply do not have in our possession or control
either what he needs or what he asks. But recognition
of the nonlegalistic character of this command—that it
is not simply a definition of external behavior to be
literally conformed to—does not mean that it fails to
lay on us a quite definite, and very demanding, obligation. When the needy man confronts me, I am to do
my utmost to help him, thinking not at all of myself,
only of him. I am not to stop short of giving him all I
possess if by doing so I can serve him in his total need,
expressed and unexpressed. Nothing less than this is
meant by this command of Jesus. Its immediate context,
not to speak of the character of Jesus' teaching as a
whole, makes this clear.

Now I venture to say that our reaction to this command thus understood is a double one. On the one hand
we find ourselves at the deepest level responding to it
with a glad assent. "Yes, this is what I am to do. The
man has asked for something he needs; I have what he
has asked for; I shall give it to him, along with myself,
my whole self. In doing so I am doing what I really
ought to do, but I am also doing what I really want to
do; I am acting in accordance with what I know to be
the true character of my life; I am being my real self.
To turn away from him would be to turn away from
happiness and peace, that ultimate happiness and peace
which I have never really known but whose existence
as a possibility I realize in moments of opportunity like

this." Such a response to Jesus' command—which, I say, is natural, belongs to our created nature and is present in some degree in every man—is what Paul had in mind when he said, "I delight in the law of God, in my inmost self" (Rom. 7:22).

But this is not our whole response to the situation in which we are placed by confrontation with the needy man. Moved by a deep impulse to give gladly and lavishly, we find ourselves hesitating and drawing back. We begin to ask questions. Some of our questions are suggested by what Paul calls "the law of sin which dwells in [our] members"; but by no means all of them need to be so explained, or indeed can be. Some of them seem to arise inevitably out of our human weakness and finitude and some of them out of a realization of our relations with and responsibilities for others. But whatever their source or however mixed their sources, we ask such questions as: "Am I willing to accept the sacrifices which love for this man and all his needy fellows would require of me? Indeed, *could* I give up so much? Am I capable of such a complete denial of self? Having always had certain satisfactions, am I actually able voluntarily to surrender them? Even if in a generous moment I did surrender them, would I be able in the long run to sustain the absence of them? And what about my obligation to my family? Even if I am ready to forget myself, can I forget them? What right have I to give to this man what belongs, not to me alone, but also to them? And what about the future? Must I not provide with savings against the time when I shall be able to support neither my family nor myself? Would I be acting responsibly, or even truly generously, if I allowed my impulse to help this man to blind me to these important obligations?" Such questions we ask inevitably, and some of them very reasonably and properly. And our answers, also inevitable and some of them also both reasonable and proper, have the effect of binding and thwarting the generous self-denying impulse, so that although we recognize the law of God and the law of our own nature in Jesus' command, "Give to him who begs of you," and find ourselves "delighting" in it in our "inmost self," it soon appears that we are both unwilling and unable actually to obey it.

It is in this position that Hamlin Garland thinks of himself as standing in the familiar poem referred to near the beginning of this book.[16] At his door a "tramp" confronts him, representing for him all the world's poverty (of whatever kind) and "its sadness." He wants "to be just"; but what is he to do? Must he give the ring from his hand? "Shall I tear off each luminous thing?" he asks. His "heart is aflame to be right." But who will tell him how to be? He calls on "those in the light" to "teach" him. Now this appeal for help is addressed to the enlightened, to the wise men, rather than to God, not because the speaker does not believe in God or because he despairs of any answer from him, but because God has already spoken. It is because the poet has already heard in his heart God's answer to his question (namely, "Give to him who begs from you") that he asks the same question of the teachers, and asks it

58

with such terrible earnestness: "What shall I do to be just?" He is only too well aware of his ultimate duty; it is because he is not able (or willing) to do that duty that he can speak, as he does, of his "sorrow and madness" and call on "the Seers" to "chart the difficult main." In other words, the poignant question for him and for all of us is: "What ought I to do in view of the fact that what I know to be my ultimate duty I cannot do?"

Thus we are brought back to the teaching problem we were considering at the end of the first chapter—the problem created by the fact that the New Testament makes no real attempt to answer that question.

When this lack or silence in the New Testament was referred to earlier, it was attributed to the "irresponsible" character of earliest Christianity, to the fact that the Christians were in New Testament times a tiny minority without political power or social influence. But it might also have been ascribed to the eschatological world view of the primitive church, to which reference has several times been made. History was soon to end, and all historical orders were shortly to be overthrown. The duty of the Christians was to be faithful to the new way in their individual lives and to maintain their unity with one another; it was not their duty either to change the social order where it was wrong or to defend it where it was right. The interim before the kingdom of God should come was so short that any acceptance of responsibility for society was out of the

question. The situation was not that social responsibility of this kind was considered but then, on reflection,
rejected; it did not come into view at all, even as a
possibility. God was going to deal with the social order;
he was going to do so decisively and soon. There is
therefore a large class of ethical questions confronting
the responsible person in every age with which the
New Testament does not directly deal.

Still another explanation, or partial explanation, of
this silence can be suggested. The New Testament presupposes and takes for granted the Old Testament. This
is a point which Jewish critics frequently ignore. Thus,
when Klausner, arguing that the New Testament ethic
fails to "embrace the whole of life" and that the law,
the prophets, and the writings of the older canon con-
tain much of indispensable value which Jesus' teaching,
or indeed the New Testament as a whole, does not
supply, offers as "proof" of his contentions the fact that
Christianity "in addition to the New Testament was
forced to accept unchanged the whole of the Old Testament as canonical Scripture" [17]—when he offers this
"proof," he gives (without intending to do so) at least
a part of the Christian's answer. Let it be granted with
Klausner that the New Testament alone is not enough,
"does not suffice"; one must go on to recognize that the
New Testament has never stood alone. There was never
a time when the church did not possess and treasure the
Old Testament. The New Testament was added to the
Old; not the Old to the New. The New Testament ethic
has its roots in prophetism and Pharisaism; and, in its

60

true mind, the church has never thought of denying that connection. Jesus came to fulfill the law and the prophets, and undoubtedly stood closer to the Pharisees than to any other group in Jewry. Paul called himself a Pharisee, and a study of his background [18] will disclose how near at a surprising number of points Paul's theology was to contemporary and traditional Jewish thought. For all his dependence upon Hellenism, Paul was more Jew than Greek, and he takes for granted the ethic of Judaism.

The accepting of the Jewish scriptures as the scriptures of the church was so much a matter of course that no one at first thought of justifying it. Later, when a corpus of Christian writings had achieved the status of scripture, the body of the church did not follow the Marcionites in substituting it for the Jewish scriptures, but rather placed it beside the other canon as the second "Testament." A sound historical instinct was manifestly at work here: the Christian church did grow out of—was continuous with—the community of Israel, and that fact was too much a fact to be denied. But a sound ethical and theological insight was also involved in this rejection of Marcionism. The church refused to separate God from the natural world; it insisted on holding together, however difficult it might be, the conception of the moral perfection of God and the conception of him as actually working in and through nature and history. The Old Testament more explicitly, but not more surely, than the New does hold these conceptions to-

61

gether and thus helps indispensably in maintaining the basis of an ethical religion.

These considerations, obviously of importance for the teaching of the early church, are not without relevance for the understanding of Jesus' own ethical teaching. It is interesting to speculate upon the extent to which Jesus was taking for granted in his teaching not only the Old Testament, but also the ongoing Jewish community with its norms and standards. Reference has already been made to Jesus' reply to a man who brought to him a quarrel with a brother over an inheritance: "Who made me a judge or divider over you?" Jesus does not want to concern himself with this problem because he sees that it is not the fundamental problem; the man's covetousness is the basic difficulty and Jesus speaks directly to it. But although he did not want to be a judge or divider, it is most unlikely that he would have denied that, as things were, there needed to be judges and dividers. Jesus' teachings, lifted out of life, are "abstractions," as a critic quoted earlier has charged; but why should they be lifted out of life? They were originally given to living men in a living community, and an understanding of that community—its history, its standards, its ways—is necessary to an understanding of the meaning of the teachings. Jesus assumed the existence of the society in which he lived, with its customs and laws. Of some of these he was very critical, and he would have refused, in any case, to identify them with the pure will of God; but it is doubtful that he contemplated even the possibility of an historical order without such standards. Jesus says on occasion that Moses gave a certain teaching because of the "hardness of [men's] hearts." Jesus challenges such teachings as representing much less than God requires. But would he have denied the fact that so long as men's hearts were hard, such teachings were needed?

If these several considerations are sound, it may be well to make a distinction between the question of the truth of the New Testament's ethical teaching and the question of its adequacy. As regards truth, we may reaffirm what was said at the end of the preceding chapter: our own hearts tell us, not only that it is true, but also that anything less strenuous and exacting could not be really and ultimately true. But as regards adequacy, if we mean by that term effectiveness in providing all the help we wish for and need in the ethical dilemmas we face as finite, sinful men in a finite and sinful world, then I believe we must acknowledge that the teaching of Jesus, and of the early church, in and of itself is not adequate. As to whether this "inadequacy" is a defect or an essential element in its strength, we shall consider briefly at a later point. That it exists I see no possible way of denying.

To recognize this fact is to recognize the necessity of a Christian casuistry, and particularly the responsibility of the Christian teacher to give help to people seeking the best possible way in situations where the perfect way cannot be followed, either because it is not open to them at all or because they lack the moral and

63

spiritual resources to follow it. Such a responsibility, if adequately borne, implies enormously high qualifications in the teacher. Not only must he be keenly sensitive to the full demand of the New Testament ethic and understand the ethical implications of membership in the body of Christ, but he must also know how devout and thoughtful Christians in various generations have found it possible to express in actual deeds their submission to the law of love, even though they, no more than we, could obey it perfectly. He must be able to draw upon the ethical insights of prophets, poets, and teachers of all cultures and traditions. He must know the world he and his hearers live in—the political, economic, social, and intellectual environment in which all ethical decisions must be made and all ethical actions taken. And not only must he know all one can know of the human heart, but he must also understand the particular persons whom he is to teach, the particular limitations within which they must act, and the particular problems they face.

The Christian teacher, in other words, is in his own way a priest—mediating between the ultimate ethical meaning of God's love for us in Christ and the human possibilities of response. As such he carries an awesome responsibility, and it goes without saying that no one is worthy or able fully to bear it. He will be comforted to some degree by the reflection that he does not stand alone. Just as the ancient Jewish teacher stood in a legal tradition and could rely on the codified results of the reflections and decisions of earlier teachers, so the

64

Christian teacher stands in his own tradition of ethical wisdom, which, although it cannot have for him the authority the law had for the Jew, can give him guidance and support. We have often been blind, not only to the necessity of a Christian casuistry, but also to our necessary dependence upon a tradition of casuistry. Even the independent Paul can speak of the Corinthian Christians as "maintaining" the "traditions" he has "delivered" to them—and one must suppose, especially in view of the context of this passage (I Cor. 11:2), that, at least in part, he has ethical traditions in mind. It is worth noting also that in this same letter, where Paul appears chiefly in the role of an ethical teacher, he distinguishes not only between the "word of the Lord" and his own "judgment," but also between both and "the practice . . . of the churches of God." The teacher does not stand alone; he is not a free lance. He represents an historical and universal community, and his teaching will be in large part the teaching of the church. All of this is true and must not be forgotten. And yet the teacher's responsibility is scarcely less awesome on this account. His task must be freshly done in every generation, indeed, in every new historical or personal situation. Ultimately the decision of what, if anything, is to be said in any particular moment must be his. Like Paul he must rely finally on his own informed and (he will pray) inspired "judgment."

I cannot go further in describing the task of the teacher in answering (or better, in helping others to

65

answer for themselves) the kind of questions we have been considering—that is, questions about what we are to do when we see that what ultimately ought to be done we cannot do. I have briefly indicated the general nature of this task and have spoken of its indispensability and of its extreme difficulty. One question about it remains to be considered, although it has never been far from our sight in this discussion—a most perplexing question, but one so central and crucial that some attempt at answering it must be made.

This is the question of the status and authority of the practicable, mediatorial counsels of the teacher, whether they are peculiarly his own and are related to a unique personal or historical situation, or whether they are derived from a tradition of how similar situations have earlier been dealt with. Can these counsels, even the best and wisest of them, be identified with the will of God? This, as I have said, is a most perplexing question. If we answer Yes, we are denying, it would seem, the validity of God's demand for perfect obedience to the law of love. If we answer No, we seem to be saying that God has nothing to say to us as we confront the necessity of decisions between greater and lesser goods or between greater and lesser evils in the actual circumstances of our lives. William Temple once stated the poignant issue:

God wills love. But does this mean that where love fails He has no care for what happens? It is because the world is a "fallen" world and has not corresponded with His

66

will for it, that the special problems of Christian conduct arise. Has God no will for His people except that they should live in a fallen world as if it were not fallen? or that being fallen themselves, they should behave outwardly as if they were not? [19]

When the question is put in this way, one's first impulsive response is likely to be: "Of course, God must have a will *for us*—for us as the particular persons we are and in our particular situations—a will adapted to our needs and possibilities." If this is true, however, what happens to the "absolute will of God"—to what Temple has in mind when he says, "God wills love"? It is hardly possible to ascribe to God two wills—that is, two wills *for us*. Either his will for us is the relative will suited to our capacities for obedience—in which case the "absolute will" becomes an abstraction; or else his will for us is the absolute will soaring far above our capacities for obedience—in which case our practicable counsels, however devout and wise, must be identified as the decisions of men. The choice between these two alternatives is a hard one, but it seems clear to me that a choice needs to be made and almost equally clear that the only possible alternative is the second of them. We have no right to identify as the will of God anything short of perfect obedience to the law of love.

My reasons for taking this position are two, both of which have been touched on more than once before. The first is that I find it impossible to regard the perfect law of love as the abstraction which the first of the two

67

alternatives necessarily implies that it is; I know myself actually to stand under its demand, and I cannot persuade myself that I am ultimately subject to any lower standard. And the second reason is really the same one, obversely stated: I cannot conceive as a possibility in this life perfect obedience to the will of God—but such obedience becomes a possibility once God's will itself is defined in terms of what is actually possible for us. In this connection, it is interesting to observe that although, as we have seen, Jesus, when confronted with the presence in the law of counsels falling far short of perfection, was able to understand, and perhaps in a measure to tolerate, them as owing to the "hardness" of men's hearts (Mark 10:3; Matt. 19:8), he does not, definitely and explicitly, ascribe them to God. "Moses allowed you . . . ," he says, "but from the beginning it was not so."

To affirm, as I believe we are forced to do, the absoluteness of God's will does not mean asserting that God has nothing to say to us in the concrete situations in which we are called on to make decisions between greater or lesser evils or goods. For God's perfect law, although it cannot be fully obeyed, does not fail to lay its demand upon us in every actual moment. One is not less under obligation to do what one can because one cannot do all one ought. God's truth will challenge, guide, and judge us; and his mercy will be not only our consolation, but also our strength. In the next chapter we shall be turning more directly to this "interim" word of God and to the relationship of truth and mercy within it. But I see no alternative to denying that we can identify any compromising moral action, however wise or necessary from our point of view, with the will of God.

I would not argue that all our moral actions are of this "compromising" kind or that within many limited situations where we are faced with the necessity of simple decisions between acting truly, equitably, or generously on the one hand, or falsely, unjustly, or meanly on the other, it is not possible for us to know clearly what is God's will and also to obey it. A judge, for example, who is offered a bribe will probably have no doubt that it is his duty under God to reject it and will also often find it within his moral power to do so. It would be arbitrary, I think, to say that in none of the moral situations in which we may stand is it possible for us to act with a good conscience. But we must be very careful in our judgments here. The matter is not nearly so simple as it may seem at first. How pure are our motives when in such a "limited" situation we make the right decision? And—an even more basic question— is it not somewhat specious to limit situations in this way? The Good Samaritan, we say, acted rightly toward the wounded stranger. But what about his part in the social neglect which accounted for the latter's plight? And what about all the other needy men whom the Good Samaritan might so easily have found if he had been making any search for them? Would he have called *himself* the "good" Samaritan?

Similarly, it may be granted that the judge did his

duty in rejecting the bribe. But *why* did he reject it? Were his motives entirely unmixed with considerations of self-interest? And was this his whole duty? Is he free from all responsibility for the prevalence of the corruption which led to the offer of the bribe? And what about his obligation of love toward the man who offered it? Is it conceivable that he has fully discharged *this* obligation? Has he the right, then, to rest content, to congratulate himself, to say, "I have done all that was required of me, not only in the sight of men, but also in the sight of God"? Would not the complacency and pride expressed in such a statement be wrong basically because the statement itself is untrue? This must not be taken to mean that before God the difference between a corrupt judge and a just one is wiped out. It does mean, however, that neither the one nor the other is in position to assert his righteousness in God's presence.

It is natural that we should want to hear God's will for us formulated in practicable terms; here is one reason for the joy the ancient Jew found in "the Law"; God had not left him in uncertainty as to what he ought to do but had told him precisely and clearly. But men have never been able indefinitely to hold on to such certainty and security. Some deep sense of the heights and depths of God's righteousness keeps breaking through the comfortable limits of our codes, forcing us to realize that they are indeed *our* codes, that they are, after all, the "traditions of men." The New Testament teaching has the virtue of being preoccupied with these heights and depths, with seeking to state the

70

pure will of God. This is its great strength; and perhaps, instead of "blaming" the social irresponsibility and the eschatological world view of the early church for its failure to deal realistically with certain particular problems of individual and social ethics, we should gratefully acknowledge that it was, humanly speaking, only because of its freedom from care about the present world that it could see so clearly what God ultimately requires, could declare it with such purity and boldness, and could thus give us an ethic so timelessly and universally relevant.

When we decide that we "ought" to act in ways which fall short of the full demands of love, we do so on our own responsibility, not God's. It may appear that by giving us freedom and by placing us in such a world as this, God requires that we take this responsibility; and, of course, once we assume it and make what seems to us to be the best possible, or the only possible, decision, we do become subject to an absolute demand which we *can* fulfill, namely, God's demand for integrity, for faithfulness to duty as we see it. Such faithfulness, within the limits set, *is* a possibility for us. But we cannot identify "duty as we see it" with God's full and perfect will for us. We may be wisely deciding what we must do or the furthest limit of what we can do; but even in the moment of such a decision about our "duty," we are aware of an ultimate demand—haunting, challenging, disturbing—which calls us beyond the actual present possibilities and denies us the luxury of contentment with ourselves. Having done what we must do, having done all we can do, we still know that we fall far short of God's perfect will for us and that we must rely on his mercy.

This mercy, offered so urgently and in such abundance, while it atones for our failures and dissolves away our guilt, does not have the effect of reducing the ethical obligation under which we stand. The fact that God is ready to give us much more than we can ask does not mean that he is not also asking for much more than we can give. This mercy of God, particularly as it bears upon the continuing validity of ethical obligation, is to be the theme of the final two chapters of this book.

Casuistry

The Ethic and the Gospel of Grace

Reference
was made at the beginning of the preceding chapter to
the only kind of peace it is given us to have—a peace
consisting, not in satisfaction that we have fulfilled God's
requirements, but in our assurance of his love, which
bears all things with us and for us. This is the "peace
of God, which passes all understanding." It is indeed
a strange, inexplicable peace—for how can God both
really require and really forbear?—but it is not strange
in the sense of being unfamiliar. Our natural human
life is not without glimpses and hints of this peace of
God—how could it be otherwise when God made us
and made us for himself? Jesus' recognition of this fact
appears in his calling God "Father" and speaking of
the family as a type of the kingdom of God. The security
and peace we have in our homes is not the peace of
knowing we are the sons and daughters, the fathers and
mothers, the husbands and wives we *ought* to be—if we
have any true sense of the obligations of family life we

shall know that we are not—but is rather the peace of knowing that our failures are not held against us. We are at rest, not because we suppose we deserve the love that surrounds us—no one who loves ever finds himself worthy of love, whether man's or God's—but because we know that whatever is lacking in our merit will be more than filled up by the grace of those who love us and whom we love. But if this is true of the relative peace we find in our homes, how much more is it true of the absolute and ultimate peace we can find only in God. If we cannot hope to deserve the love of those who after all ask so little of us, how can we deserve the love of him who asks so much? The whole meaning of the Christian gospel is that we do not need to deserve it; that he who asks everything stands ready and is able to give us all things. But this is the mystery of all love, and only in a supreme sense and measure, of the love of God.

Now, as I have already hinted, this conclusion may seem at first sight to have the effect of cutting the nerve of moral effort and of destroying the whole ground on which the teacher of ethics must stand. We considered earlier the objection of certain Jewish critics that Jesus' ethical teaching had the effect of discouraging moral endeavor by virtue of its sheer impossibility. That objection may seem now to be confirmed and even reinforced: "Why try to be worthy," one may ask, "if I know, not only that I cannot be, but also that I do not need to be? If God's favor toward me is a matter of pure grace, what incentive do I have for fulfilling the ethical demands we have been considering? Indeed, do not the ethical demands themselves cease to be demands? Are not their force and reality abrogated and destroyed?" The other questions as to the soundness of the Christian ethic came from outside of the church; this one comes from inside. It is, moreover, a more radical and searching question than any of the others because it strikes, not at Jesus' ethic only, but at the reality and authority of *any* ethic as binding on the Christian. How will the Christian teacher answer this question? How shall we deal with this most serious challenge, not only to the authority of Jesus' ethical teaching, but also to the authority of the moral law in any form?

We shall deal with it, I should say, by pointing to the fact that God's act in accepting us is an act of forgiveness and that forgiveness in its very nature presupposes the acknowledgment of, and submission to, a moral requirement. This is the answer clearly, if implicitly, given in Jesus' teaching and confirmed in our own experience; and we shall shortly consider it. It is an answer so obvious, once God's act is identified as a *forgiving* act, that I venture to say the question would never have arisen in the church if Paul had not interpreted God's act in another way. Paul identified God's saving act as an act of *justification,* and in doing so, as I see it, set grace and law against each other in a way that seriously distorts both Jesus' teaching and the realities of the Christian's experience. It is not an accident that the only places in the New Testament where the antinomian question is explicitly raised are in Paul's letters. Paul quotes his opponents as raising it and, of course, vigorously and with indubitable sincerity, repudiates the ascription of antinomian implications to his doctrine; but I do not believe that we can deny the fact of these implications, however remote they may be from Paul's intention. Paul's doctrine of justification has in itself the seeds of antinomianism, and Paul's critics, or perhaps heretical followers, were not being merely perverse in saying so.

It is not unusual for students of Paul to interpret justification in his usage as the equivalent of forgiveness. In a sense, of course, that is true: he is referring to the divine act which leads to our reconcilation with God. In other words, justification takes the place in Paul's presentation of the gospel which forgiveness occupies in Jesus' teaching. But that is not to say that "justification" is a word of identical, or even of synonymous, meaning. Indeed, taken at its face value, justification means something very different indeed. The term "justify" in English means to establish as just or true, to vindicate, or to acquit. One who says, "I have been justified," means: "I have been proved right. It has been established (whether in the light of a fuller knowledge of the circumstances, or through later developments, or in a court of some kind) that my words (or acts) were right and proper. My judgment (or my statement, or my conduct, as the case may be) has been vindicated." Obviously, one does *not* mean, "I have been forgiven." "Forgiveness" presupposes that one was in the wrong;

"justification," that one was in the right. That this is the situation *in English* is manifestly true. But what about the word "justify" in Greek, and particularly in the Greek of the Septuagint and of Paul? It is argued that "to be justified" has there a richer, more complicated meaning—some such meaning as "to be brought into right relations, to be set right, with God." But even if this be granted, the question still remains as to the more precise character of God's justifying act. *How* does he bring us into right relations with himself? Surely, *we* would say, by forgiving us. But the Greek word for justify—any more than the English word— does not suggest that this answer is expected. The word is primarily a legal, forensic term, and its meaning is predominantly, neither to "make upright," nor yet to "forgive," but to "pronounce righteous," to "place in a legally right position." Although one does not need to claim that Paul is always consistent, there is every reason to conclude that this is predominantly its meaning for him.

Now it is clear that, having conceived of God's primary saving act as a *justifying* act, Paul finds himself in a logical difficulty. Legal justification would seem to be possible only on the basis of obedience to law. A violator of the law cannot, in the nature of the case, be justified. But every man is such a violator. Paul devotes the first several chapters of Romans to demonstrating the universal sinfulness of mankind, to proving the conclusion that by the law no flesh is justified. And yet the believer *is* justified. How can this be? One might think

77

that this apparent contradiction would have led Paul to examine his term again—is "justification" the proper way to think of the new status of the believer? Actually, however, it led him to repudiate the law entirely as a factor in justification. In Christ is manifested a way of justification apart from law altogether. We are justified on the basis of faith in Christ. To be sure, the law is not entirely out of the picture: it is the failure of our attempts to keep the law which drives us in despair to avail ourselves of God's offer of release from the law through Christ, and it is what Christ has done to the law which makes possible that offer of release. Paul evidently thought of Christ's act, as regards its relation to the law, in various, and not always consistent, ways. Sometimes, his point seems to be that Christ offered the perfect obedience to the law which we could not give and thus broke the law's power over us; sometimes, it appears that Christ has paid the penalty of our disobedience to the law and thus freed us from its threat; sometimes, it seems almost as though the law is hypostatized or personalized, being conceived of as one of the great enemies of mankind along with sin and death, and that Christ has met this power in some kind of battle and has defeated and destroyed him. But however this action of Christ is *conceived,* its effect is to break the hold of law upon those who place their trust in him. God saves us, according to Paul, not in the first instance by dealing with *us* as transgressors, but by dealing with the law which makes us such. We are saved *from* it; we are not saved *under* it. We are set right with

God, put into correct formal relations with him (justified), not because we are found to have kept the law, nor yet because we have been forgiven for breaking it, but because the law itself has been rendered invalid for us. This is, of course, only the first step. The legal obstacles having been removed through our justification or acquittal, God can now become our "Father" and enter into personal relations with us as his "sons" (it is significant that Paul uses a legal term "adoption" to describe even our sonship). We are now reconciled. We may know the joy and peace of the Spirit, God's very presence in love. But this reconciliation has been made possible by a prior, more completely objective, dealing, through Christ and particularly through the Cross, with "the bond which stood against us with its legal demands" (Col. 2:14). A victory has been won and a release has been accomplished for us—a release, not only from sin and death, but also, and in a sense first of all, from law. Thus, I say, the doctrine of justification has inescapable antinomian implications.[20]

But the truth of the matter is that justification is not the most apt way of representing the meaning of God's act in Christ in its bearing upon our plight as guilty sinners. Forgiveness is the more appropriate term. This is not to reduce our situation in Christ to something merely individual or subjective. God did act objectively in Christ, laying the ground for our reconciliation. But this objective act was not the abrogating of the law so that we could be "justified"; it was rather the creating of the church, the new community of grace, in which we can know the meaning of forgiveness. It must be recognized, of course, that no human term can be entirely adequate to describe God and his acts. All of our terms, when applied to God, are metaphorical. But some metaphors are more adequate than others; and the truest metaphors of God's relationship with us and of ours with him are provided by the life of the family, as we have seen. "Forgiveness" is such a metaphor. "We are forgiven" is a truer statement of our situation in Christ than is "We are justified." And forgiveness does not involve release from law, but pardon under law and the restoration of fellowship under law. In forgiveness the authority of law is fully validated, even in the moment when our guilt is done away. Once we think of God's saving act as a forgiving act, as Jesus did, and conceive of our relationship with him, from start to finish, as finding its truest human analogy in the life of the family—once we do this, the problem Paul struggled with disappears, though the wonder and the mystery remain.

I have already referred to the parables in the fifteenth chapter of Luke. One of them particularly is bound to come to our minds when we consider the place and meaning of grace in Jesus' teaching, the parable of the Prodigal Son; and it will be illuminating to consider it in this connection.

The main point of this parable, at least as the Evangelist understands it, is indicated clearly enough by the context in which it has been placed. Just as a shepherd rejoices more over the one sheep that has been lost than over the ninety-nine which did not stray away and just as the woman is happier at finding the one coin she had lost than she had been in simply possessing the nine coins still left to her, so the father in this story is happier over the younger son who has returned than over the older son who did not go away. Thus also there is more joy in heaven "over one sinner who repents than over ninety-nine righteous persons who need no repentance."

But although the principal point of the story in its present context is thoroughly clear, we cannot be sure that such was its original context in Jesus' teaching. Matthew has the parable of the lost sheep in a different setting and does not have the parable of the lost son at all. Besides, the analogy between the parables of the sheep and the coins on the one hand and the parable of the sons on the other is by no means exact or complete. The main difference lies in the fact that whereas the sheep and the coins are quite inert and only the shepherd and the woman are significantly active, in the third parable both sons, as well as their father participate decisively and in different ways in the action of the story. Thus, whether we think of this story in close connection with the other two or not, we cannot avoid finding a far wider and deeper range of meaning in this great story than the one point which the context brings into focus, and this can be done without the slightest measure of allegorizing. Indeed, the parable illustrates with amazing aptness the whole aspect of Jesus' teaching which we are now considering.

One comes, I think, nearest to understanding the heart of the story when one observes how the conceptions of son and slave or "hired servant" keep appearing in various connections.[21] More than once one is reminded of the vast superiority in status of the son to the servant. The young man says, "I am no longer worthy to be called your son; treat me as one of your hired servants." Likewise, the slaves are ordered to bring out the robe, the ring, and the fatted calf for the son, even for this son. Even this renegade son is better than the slaves. Any son who is really a son is better than any slave. I say "who is really a son," meaning a son who knows what it is to be a son, who shares in the love which unites the family, who knows that he stands under a heavier obligation than any code of rules could possibly embody or than any obedience of his could possibly discharge, who knows that he must rely upon the forgiveness of others rather than upon his own merit, and because he knows himself to be in need of forgiveness and to be in fact forgiven is able to forgive. Such is a son, and however far he may wander from his father's house, he has a place there—and in his father's heart—which no slave or "hired servant" can ever claim. The younger man in this story is a son—a prodigal son, but still a son. When he says "I am no longer worthy to be called your son," he shows that he knows what it means to be a son, and one can know that only by being one.

82

But his older brother is a slave. Listen to him: "Lo, these many years I have served you, and I never disobeyed your command; yet you never gave me a kid, that I might make merry with my friends." The younger man is a son who now realizes that he is not worthy of being even a slave in his father's house; the older man is a slave who supposes that because he is a good slave he is worthy of being a son and wonders why his father does not treat him so.

The father wants to treat him so: "Son," he says to him, "you are always with me and all that is mine is yours." But he cannot treat him as a son. The man himself will not permit it. He prefers to be a slave and thus to be able proudly to say, "I never disobeyed your command," than to be a son and have to say, "I have sinned . . . I am no longer worthy." But he cannot have it both ways. The slave can have the satisfaction of knowing that he has done his full duty as a slave, but he cannot know the rewards of sonship. The son, who can never be satisfied that he has done his full duty as a son, can know the deeper satisfaction of being a son, that is, of being forgiven, of being at home with those who love him and whom he loves.

It is not the father who refuses this deeper satisfaction to the elder son; it is this son who is unable to claim it. He does not even want it. He now refuses to come in, even though the fatted calf has been killed and he is being urged by his father himself to join his family in eating it. His interests are outside of the family alto-

83

gether. "You never gave *me* a kid," he says, "that I might make merry with *my* friends."

It is this son only who finds fault with his father for treating the younger brother otherwise than on the basis of merit. The father has acted as a father characteristically acts; but the older brother, since he does not know what it means to be a son, cannot understand what it means to be a father. To him his father's action seems not only unjust, but utterly irresponsible, arbitrary, and perverse—like paying everybody the same wage, no matter how little or how much each has worked. But to anyone who is a father (or for that matter any member of a true family) the joyous receiving of the penitent Prodigal will not seem unjust, although such a one will not find himself thinking of it, either, as just or even as generous; he will think of it simply as being quite perfectly appropriate. It is just the way a father acts—not logical perhaps, but true. And Jesus is saying to us that in this which is most familiar we touch the mystery of the kingdom of God; that deep in what we know best and most intimately the secret of the meaning of our existence is hidden, and revealed.

Of course, repentance is necessary—whether we are thinking of life in the home or life with God. But repentance is no arbitrary condition; it is simply realization. Repentance is facing up to the facts about ourselves and taking appropriate action. Repentance is not remorse, or even, in a primary degree, regret or sorrow, however sincere and deep-going. It is interesting that

84

in this story of Jesus not a word is said about any regret or sorrow on the son's part. This does not mean that he was not sorry; undoubtedly he was. It does mean, however, that such sorrow is not the essential, the really significant, thing about repentance. Repentance is not primarily the emotion of regret, but the act of realization: "He came to himself." He faced up to the facts about himself. He realized what he had done to his father and sensed the full bitter meaning of that severing of fellowship with his father for which his own selfish and rash act had been responsible. If the process of realization had stopped there, the end would have been remorse and despair; but it did not stop there, midway. He realized that his father's house was still there and that his only hope of any security and peace lay there, in however menial a position. He realized not only what he had done, but also what he might and must now do. He arose and came to his father. That is repentance. There is faith and hope and action in it, as well as sorrow.

But the fact that there is faith and hope in repentance does not mean that transgression is taken less seriously than would otherwise be true. One might argue that the children of an unselfish and forgiving parent will be more disobedient than those of a harsh and selfish one, but we know that this is not true. It is the very fact that I know my father unselfishly cares for me which makes disobedience the ugly thing it is. It is not that I have broken his rules and thus hurt his pride—I might feel a certain pride of my own in doing that—but that I

85

have hurt his trust in me and have separated myself from his love for me. Such, in an incalculably deeper sense, is the meaning of our disobedience to God. One to whom a knowledge of God's forgiveness has been vouchsafed in Christ will not take God's will less seriously on that account, but immeasureably more seriously.

Such repentance is absolutely necessary if there is to be reconciliation between human beings or between men and God. This necessity belongs to our very nature as persons. The most striking difference among the three parables of Luke 15 is that whereas the coin must wait till the woman finds it and the sheep till the shepherd comes, in the third story, it is the father who waits. He is just as eager as the shepherd and the woman could possibly be, but he is dealing, not with a coin or a sheep, but with his son; he must wait. He must wait till he sees him coming—afar off, it is true, but coming. Only then is his eagerness freed of all bounds, as he runs to meet him, falls on his neck, and kisses him; only then does the initiative in the story pass from the son to the father. It is he who, breaking short his son's apologies, calls for the robe and the ring and the fatted calf. Of course, we may argue that the initiative rested with the father all the time; it was the memory of his home which drew the son back. But just as he had deliberately left, so now he must deliberately return.

Those who find an antinomian tendency in the Christian doctrine of grace, who say, "Let us then sin that

grace may abound," who ask, "Why should we try to
fulfill God's law when we know not only that we cannot
succeed, but also that God stands ready graciously to
receive us even in our sinfulness?" or who take the even
more radical position of saying, "Christ has destroyed
the law,"—all of these (and, I think, Paul is included
here) forget or neglect the great significance of repentance in the Christian doctrine of grace.

Forgiveness is a reality with two sides, and one side
is penitence. Not only is there no forgiveness without
repentance; in the nature of things there cannot be.
But if it is clear that we cannot be forgiven without
repenting, it is equally clear that we cannot repent
unless we take seriously the ethical demands under
which we stand. One cannot live repentantly who does
not seek to live justly and lovingly. Moreover, the
degree in which we can know the meaning of God's
forgiveness—and we can know that meaning in many
degrees—depends upon the measure of our repentance
and therefore upon the measure of the moral seriousness of our living. The more strenuously and faithfully
we *try* to live, the more genuine and thoroughgoing our
penitence can be, and the larger our capacity for receiving the forgiveness of God. To become ethically in-
different is to lose our power to repent, and to lose our
power to repent is the only possible way of finally losing
our souls. The unforgivable sin is the sin for which we
are no longer able to be contrite and from which we are
no longer able even to desire to turn away.

Repentance, then, is not a merely verbal act which

we occasionally perform; if real, it is an act in which our whole selves through the whole course of our lives are strenuously involved. It is not a casual "Sorry," any more than God's forgiveness is a casual "Not at all." Just as God's forgiveness of us is so serious that we can find an adequate symbol of it only in the dying on a cross of the Son of his love, so repentance in its true character is a concern about our sin so radical as to break up the deeps of our souls and so creative as to commit us, body and spirit, to an unwithholding sacrifice of devotion and obedience.

Family obligations in far more binding than any moral laws.

The Ethic and the Life of the Spirit

In the preceding chapter we were considering the place of moral obligation in the experience of being forgiven. We saw that the recognition of obligation and earnest effort to discharge it are necessary prerequisites of forgiveness. In this final chapter I should like to make a similar point about the character of the righteousness which ideally follows upon repentance and forgiveness—the point, namely, that moral seriousness and strenuous moral effort are the necessary presuppositions of any goodness it may be given one to have. I say "given one to have," because it must be recognized that just as forgiveness is God's gift, so is the highest kind of righteousness. It is God's endowment, not our achievement. Thus, the antinomian question is raised again and in a somewhat different form: "Since it is true not only that I cannot attain goodness by my own effort but also that God stands ready to bestow goodness upon me, why should I make any moral effort at all?"

Again, I think it is true to say, this question can be raised with some plausibility largely because of the influence of Paul. And some further discussion of Paul's ethical teaching, particularly of how this teaching is related to his theology, is called for in this connection.

We have seen that the Synoptic Gospels sum up Jesus' ethical teaching in the term *agape,* and that this love is directed toward God and toward neighbor. Paul also often uses the same word (and its cognates). It is striking, however, that whereas Jesus never speaks of God as "loving" us, Paul rarely speaks of us as "loving" God; and, it may be added, his use of the term in the strictly ethical sense (that is, to designate an obligatory attitude or way of acting toward our neighbors) is relatively infrequent. The clearest exception (there are only two or three even possible exceptions) to the generalization that Paul does not think of us as "loving" God appears in Rom. 8:28, where he writes, "In everything God works for good with those who love him." But it is almost as though, having said "who love him," he immediately regretted the phrase and tried to atone for it, by adding, "[that is, those] who are called according to his purpose." Paul instinctively distrusts any phrase which suggests human initiative in our relation with God. "Who love him" suggests not only human initiative, but also (he would feel) even human merit; he therefore turns to the more congenial passive voice, "who are called." It is God who does both the "loving" and the "calling." Such a passage as "God shows his love for us in that while we were yet sinners Christ died for us" sets forth Paul's most frequent and characteristic use of the term "love," both noun and verb. But *agape,* for Paul, is more than an attitude of God toward us or the motive for his gracious dealings with us; it is more objective and concrete than that. It is hardly too much to say that *agape* is God himself acting in Christ. Thus Paul can speak of the love of God as "poured into our hearts." A proper distinction can doubtless be made between "love" and "grace," as Paul uses these terms; but the distinction would be a fine one, and not an altogether certain one. For most purposes and in most contexts, the two terms are interchangeable. Both represent the reality of God coming to us in Christ. In the same approximate way "love" and "Spirit" can be identified: "God's love has been poured into our hearts through the Holy Spirit which has been given to us" (Rom. 5:5) .

This love elicits a response from us, but Paul prefers not to regard this response as an answering "love" (it is the Johannine writer [I John 4:19] who can say that "we love, because he first loved us") ; the response is more appropriately (as Paul sees it) called "faith." *Love* is God's prerogative. It is true that Paul uses the term in speaking of our relations with others. But this love is not primarily ours; it is God's love "poured into our hearts" and now flowing through us like a current to others—or, to change the figure, bearing its fruits of longsuffering, kindness, and the like. The ethical fruits are set forth (as we shall see, somewhat inconsistently) in the hortatory sections of many of Paul's letters, perhaps supremely in I Corinthians 13. But even in this passage love itself is God's love, not ours. That is why it is "the greatest of [them]." "Faith" and "hope" represent human responses; "love," the reality to which the response is made.

This love working through us manifests itself in a characteristic ethical behavior—compassion, readiness to forgive, and the like—but it is more than the mere sum of these virtues; rather, it is the ground of them. It is the common life, the *koinonia*, which is expressed through them. Although Paul does not make the implication clear, it is obvious that *agape*, thus defined, belongs essentially within the Christian community and has meaning there which it cannot have outside. Paul was enough of a Jew to quote, "You shall love your neighbor as yourself," and to see in it a summary of the law. Moreover, although in Gal. 5:14 Paul quotes this commandment in a context where love within the church is being discussed, in Rom. 13:9, where the passage is again quoted, he is clearly using "neighbor" in the broader sense, to include all men. But in Gal. 6:10 he writes: "So then, as we have opportunity, let us do good to all men, and especially to those who are of the household of faith." Our first obligation is the obligation of *brotherly love* (as distinguished from neighborly love); and the primary locus of *agape* is within the community of Christ. It is because others belong within that community—or at any rate because we want them to belong to it—that *agape* moves toward them.

This identification of *agape* with the life of the Christian community is complete in the Fourth Gospel and the First Epistle of John; and if a digression can be permitted, it may be well to notice this development. "A new commandment I give to you," says Jesus (John 13:34; cf. I John 2:7 ff.), "that you love one another." It is a "new commandment" just for this reason: it prescribes the spirit of the new community. There is in the Fourth Gospel no sign of interest in those outside of the community—except, of course, in the elect who are still outside; but these actually belong to the community as certainly as do those who have already been gathered. In spite of very occasional references to "the world" as the object of God's love (John 3:16; I John 4:9 ff.), the emphasis in these writings falls on God's love of the church. In line with this emphasis is the stress on the love of God for Christ, that is, for "the Son" (John 3:35; 10:17) ; for Christ is so closely identified with those "whom the Father has given him" that to speak of God's love for the one is to speak of his love for the other. "All love finds its true center in him [Christ]; his sole function is to mediate God's love." [22] "As the Father has loved me, so have I loved you." *Agape* is the distinctive spirit of the Christian fellowship; it is the reality of God, his Spirit; it is the continuing presence, the abiding Spirit, of Christ.

It is frequently said that *agape* in the Fourth Gospel and the First Epistle of John is entirely a mystical conception, without ethical content. This is too simple a statement. It is true that love is primarily and predominantly the mystical bond of the church's unity; but it also has important ethical implications. This fact is at least implied in the Gospel and becomes explicit and emphatic in the epistle, which insists upon the duty of Christians to care for the needs of one another as forcefully as does that most simply ethical of all the New Testament books, the Epistle of James. But this duty of *agape* in the Johannine writings is, for the most part, limited to concern for other Christians. Just as *agape* belongs to the community and is not found outside, so its ethical demands are addressed to its members and apply only to other members. *Agape* is brotherly love, not neighborly love. "The world" is given up and disregarded. Love "for John . . . is the principle of the Christ-world which is being built up in the midst of the contemporary cosmic crisis";[23] and, it may be added, it is only within this new "Christ-world" (i.e., the church) that the Christian stands under ethical obligation.

It is worth saying again that an ethic having its root, as the Christian ethic at its most authentic and most distinctive undoubtedly does, in the experience of God's love in Christ—that is, in the life of the church—does not need to be thus limited. One may think of the church as potentially including all men, so that love, even brotherly love, becomes universally appropriate and obligatory: every man is a "brother for whom Christ died." Here is the distinctively Christian ground for

94

abhorring all injustice, cruelty, and neglect, not only among Christians, but among human beings generally. In every instance of man's inhumanity to man, in every denial of justice and fraternity, whether between individuals or within the structures of our social, economic, and political life, the reality of the church is being denied and violated, Christ is being crucified afresh, his body broken. Here, in the realized meaning of the church, lies the immediate source of any distinctive Christian contribution to the understanding or solution of ethical issues, individual or social. For the reality of the church cannot be limited to what it happens actually to be in any particular time and place. It is the promise—indeed, the beginning, the "firstfruits"—of the universal kingdom of God. The church as possibility —and therefore in its full and essential reality—includes, so far as we can know, all mankind.

But although all of this is implicit in the sense of the church which belongs so profoundly and pervasively to the Fourth Gospel, there is too little reason to believe that John consciously thought in this more inclusive way. Christ's "new commandment" is new, not only because the love it prescribes is new in its quality ("as I have loved you"), but also because it is neither a possibility nor an obligation except among the small and scattered elect belonging to the newly created society. One might discern a kind of circle in this development: undoubtedly in Leviticus "Love your neighbor" meant "Love your fellow Israelite"; now the corresponding "new commandment" is "Love your fellow Christian." The ethical universalism of sections of the Synoptic Gospels, not to mention the Prophets, has all but disappeared.

For Paul, however, although *agape* belongs primarily within the Christian community—indeed is virtually another name *for* that community—it clearly implies obligations toward all mankind. And Paul's conception of the nature of these obligations is very close to Jesus' own. As we have already seen in another connection, one cannot read Paul's letters with particular attention to their ethical teaching without being struck by many similarities with the recorded teaching of Jesus. Not only is Paul deeply concerned about the moral behavior of the members of his churches, resorting constantly to moral exhortations of the most earnest kind, but the quality of the ethical life he is seeking to encourage is much like that which Jesus also requires. A very general resemblance might be accounted for by the common background of both teachers in Judaism, but the similarities are too close for that to be an adequate answer. Some actual echoes of Jesus' recorded words can probably be found in Paul; but much more important than these scattered verbal reminiscences is the highly distinctive character of the ethical teaching in such passages as, say, I Corinthians 13 or Romans 12. The reader of these passages (and there are many more such) is bound to take knowledge of Paul that he has been, if not with Jesus in the flesh (which is most unlikely), then with him as he was remembered in some

96

early community. There can be no question that in this respect at least the mind of Christ was in Paul.

But clear as is Paul's recognition that Christians are under obligation to live a life of love, and faithful as he is in urging them to do so, it is not clear that his understanding of what God has done in Christ and of the corresponding status of the believer provided any adequate theoretical or theological basis for this obligation. For law in some sense is the necessary presupposition of obligation, and according to Paul, the believer is not under law—he has been set free from it, as we have seen. I say, "law in some sense," and the qualification is very important in this discussion, for the term "law" has many meanings—with Paul as with us. If the word is restricted to a definite code, a list of particular acts which are prescribed or prohibited, then obviously we have no right to say that law is the necessary ground of obligation. But throughout this discussion the term is being used in a much more inclusive sense. By "law of God" is meant God's categorical demand upon my moral life, with all that the fulfillment of that demand involves. The "law of God" is what God requires of me. Because this requirement is not fortuitous or whimsical or arbitrary, but is consistent with his nature and with the nature of his relations with me and with his creation—it is basically the same requirement of me and of all men —it can properly be called his "law." Without the assumption of the existence of some such divine re-

97

quirement one cannot talk with full conviction about human obligation.

But, it may be asked, is Paul's rejection of the law as binding on the believer so radical as this? Is not the "law" he rejects simply an external code, a list of *thou shalt's* and *thou shalt not's,* in particular the code of Judiasm? Whatever may seem to be implied in some of his practical teaching, I feel sure that in his "theory" of the Christian life Paul went much further than this. Although undoubtedly he is frequently referring to the Jewish law, one cannot deny the presence—often, if not always—of a more radical, more inclusive, reference. The Gentiles also are subject to law (Rom. 2:15) ; will they not share, with redeemed Jews, in release from the burden of its demands? And when Paul speaks of this release, can he have only an external code in mind? Would he have said, "God has freed us from a code of particular rules by making us subject to a higher, more exacting law—a law which lays its demands upon the very thoughts of our hearts and calls for an absolutely unremitting obedience?" Jesus speaks to this effect, but I do not believe Paul would have done so. Certainly he does not in fact speak so. It is striking that when, in the seventh chapter of Romans, he is telling of the difficulties he himself had under the Jewish law, he mentions particularly only the one commandment of the Decalogue which involves a demand upon the inner life, "You shall not covet." [24] Now many of us would make a significant distinction between "rules" and "principles," and would say that whereas the law in the external sense of rules is abrogated in Christ, the principles remain valid and binding. In line with this distinction we might insist that the Christian is no longer under any specific command touching outward behavior, even a command as important as "Thou shalt not kill." But would we not concede that he is still subject to the law against covetousness? But can we think of Paul as making any such concession? Would he have allowed continuing validity to the law at the very point where it had caused him the greatest pain and anxiety? There is no evidence that Paul differentiated between various elements within the law—or various kinds of law—as, for example, between the ceremonial and moral, or the general and the particular.[25] Law, as such, is no longer valid for the Christian. We are not under law, but under grace.

Such an understanding of the Christian's position left Paul, I have said, without an adequate theoretical basis for the practical ethical demands he does not fail to make upon his congregations. This lack, we may believe, caused some perplexity among his hearers, as it certainly opened the way to heretical antinomianism; and it no doubt caused Paul himself some concern. When at the beginning of Romans 6 Paul asks, "What shall we say then? Are we to continue in sin that grace may abound?" we are safe in assuming that he is not merely repeating a question his opponents have hurled at him; he has been troubled by the question himself. One notes that he does not really answer it. (Without the conception of the continuing validity of law in some sense, he *cannot* answer it.) He points to the fact that Christians are new men in Christ, that they have died with Christ to sin, and asks, "How can they still live in it?" In other words, he points to the *necessity* of righteousness in the Christian, not to the *obligation* of it. How *can* those who are "free from sin" still live in it? And yet Paul's readers undoubtedly did live in it. And so he must resort to exhortation that they shall *not* be what they (by definition) cannot be and that they *shall* be what they (by definition) cannot help being. Nygren[26] argues that when Paul in this passage (Rom. 6:1-11) affirms that the Christian is "free from sin," he does not mean that he is sinless but only that he has been set free from sin sufficiently to enable him to "fight sin." But there is absolutely nothing in the passage itself to suggest such a meaning—every sentence and phrase points the other way—and Nygren's only argument is the fact that the following paragraph of exhortation (not to mention all the practical ethical admonitions in Paul's letters generally) shows clearly that Paul is aware that his hearers are not without sin. But this is the inconsistency in Paul which we are discussing; and to assume consistency and interpret the materials accordingly is to beg the question. The fact that Paul has not really answered the antinomian's question in verse 1 of Romans 6 and that he realizes that he has not done so is manifest in verse 15, where after all his argument he asks exactly the same question again: "What then? Are we to sin because we are not under law but under grace?" At verse 15 he is precisely where he was at verse

1, and the intervening discussion, however valuable for other reasons, has been for the particular purpose irrelevant. He is precisely where he was because, I repeat, without the conception of the continuing validity of law, the antinomian's question is unanswerable. It may be rejected as abhorrent and blasphemous (Rom. 3:5-8; 6:2, 15), but it cannot be answered.

I would not argue that Paul's denial that the law is binding on the believer was absolutely constant and invariable. One can cite scattered passages in his letters where "the law" is appealed to in exhortations to his Christian readers. These passages are strikingly few, however, as compared with those in which the law is spoken of as belonging to the old aeon, which for the Christian has been left behind. Of these few the most notable, perhaps, is Rom. 13:8-10:

Owe no one anything, except to love one another; for he who loves his neighbor has fulfilled the law. The commandments, "You shall not commit adultery, You shall not kill, You shall not steal, You shall not covet," and any other commandment, are summed up in this sentence, "You shall love your neighbor as yourself." Love does no wrong to a neighbor; therefore love is the fulfilling of the law.

But even in this passage one cannot be quite sure that the continuing validity of the law *as imposing obligation*[27] is being unequivocally affirmed. Does "love is the fulfilling of the law" mean that the Christian is

101

required by God's command to love his neighbor—that he stands under this moral demand—or does it mean that in the life of *agape*, in which he shares in virtue of his membership in Christ, the law's requirement of love is inevitably fulfilled, and therefore transcended and in a real sense invalidated?

The same question can appropriately be asked about Gal. 5:13-14: "For you were called to freedom, brethren; only do not use your freedom as an opportunity for the flesh, but through love be servants of one another. For the whole law is fulfilled in one word, 'You shall love your neighbor as yourself.'" It is noteworthy that in the immediate context of this passage in Galatians Paul explicitly says, "If you are led by the Spirit you are not under the law." And that he is not thinking here of any merely "ceremonial," or even any narrowly Jewish, law would seem to be implied by his way of describing the "works of the flesh" (impurity, jealousy, selfishness, etc.), against which the law stands (but out of which the Christian has been delivered), and the "fruits of the Spirit" (love, patience, kindness, self-control, and the like), with respect to which the law is utterly irrelevant.

But it is too much to expect Paul to be absolutely consistent on such a point as this, especially when he is being hard pressed to deal effectively with the moral failures of his people; and I am not disposed to insist on any particular understanding of these paragraphs in Romans and Galatians or of a few other passages (such as I Cor. 7:19) found in various practical contexts in his letters, where the continuing binding force of law may seem to be implied. I *would* insist, however, that in whatever way these scattered passages are understood, they do not obscure the fact that, according to Paul's *theory* of the Christian life, the law belongs to the past. In the past, to be sure, it had a purpose "holy and just and good"; but for those who belong to Christ, that purpose has been served. Is not telling evidence of this to be found in Paul's total silence about the continuing necessity of repentance and our continuing need of forgiveness? He nowhere deals with the problem of what can be done about the Christian's current transgressions. Can this fact be explained on any other theory than that Paul does not envisage the possibility of transgression within the Christian life? How can we be transgressors when we are not under law? "The law was our custodian until Christ came. . . . But . . . we are no longer under a custodian" (Gal. 3:24-25). Here is Paul's characteristic teaching and, I say again, it deprives him of any adequate *theoretical* ground for his ethical admonitions to those who are in Christ. He may *exhort* them not to use their "freedom as an opportunity for the flesh," but he cannot deny the fact of the freedom itself.

Now Paul's repudiation of the law as binding upon the believer resulted not alone from his realization that it was impossible to keep it—and therefore to be saved by it or through it—and from his confidence that Christ had fulfilled the law, in the sense of fulfilling its purpose, and had thus destroyed its power; it resulted also from his insight that the highest righteousness possible for men was not the achievement of moral effort but was the free gift of God. This righteousness is an aspect of the new life in Christ or, to say the same thing differently, it is a fruit of the Spirit. We considered earlier the difficulty which many find with the teaching of Jesus that it requires love, which by its very nature must be spontaneous, not subject to the will. One cannot say to oneself, "Go to, now, I will love." And if the true righteousness is the righteousness of love, it can hardly be the consequence of obedience to law. The realization that this is true can easily have, as we have seen, the effect of undermining the authority or importance of law. This effect, we are now saying, is even more likely and plausible when it is observed—about others at least—that in some measure it is possible for one to have the righteousness of love, but that this righteousness is in fact not the result of conscious obedience to rules but comes to one as a free and undeserved gift. Authentic righteousness is God's righteousness, not one's own. It is God's love shed abroad in our hearts by the Holy Spirit which is given unto us. It is a living thing, the issue of a living process which man does not control. It is not the mechanical product of deliberate purpose. It is indeed the fruit of the Spirit.

Although we are likely to think of this emphasis upon the vital, spontaneous, nondeliberative, nonlegalistic character of the highest goodness as particularly characteristic of Paul (it is indeed one of his truest and most important insights), we must not miss the ample evidence that Jesus thought of goodness at its highest level in the same way. What else is the point of such a saying as, "If any one forces you to go one mile, go with him two miles," or "If any one would sue you and take your coat, let him have your cloak as well"? In sayings like these Jesus is certainly meaning to place us under obligation; but that is not all he is doing. He is not merely laying down rules or enunciating a mandatory principle, but is suggesting and illustrating a kind of goodness which no measure of obedience to rules or principles, however high and exacting, could possibly give. He is doing the same thing when he says that we must forgive our enemies seventy-seven times, that is, without limit. The only person who can fulfill such a requirement is the kind of person who *wants* to forgive, who *is* forgiving. This same spontaneous goodness appears particularly clearly in some of the characteristic parables in Luke's Gospel. It is certainly no sense of duty which moves the father of the Prodigal Son to receive him as he does. The extravagance of the welcome rules out that possibility. The elder brother objects because his father has gone so far beyond what any reasonable sense of obligation would have required. Or note the extravagance of the Good Samaritan, binding up the wounds of the stricken foreigner, pouring in oil and wine, setting him on his own beast, bringing him to the inn, and taking care of him. He could have stopped so much sooner than this and still have fulfilled any possible rule about one's duty to a wounded stranger. But he did not stop even then—leaving money to pay for the man's further care, and insisting that if more were needed, he should be allowed to pay the account on his return. The Good Samaritan is not trying to do his duty. The point is that he is not aware of duty at all—any more than we are aware of duty when we act generously *toward ourselves.* We act so toward ourselves because we want to; so the Samaritan acted toward the needy stranger. Is this one of the possible meanings of loving one's neighbor as oneself?

This recognition of the spontaneity, the living quality, of true goodness is, then, as characteristic of Jesus as of Paul. Perhaps we can say that it is characteristic of Paul because it was first characteristic of Jesus. With greater assurance we can say that it was characteristic of both because it is a recognition of the truth, which our own experience confirms, and particularly our experience in Christ. True goodness, wherever we meet with it, has this same quality. It is God's creation, not man's construction. There is a kind of righteousness which man can set to and make, just as there is a kind of poetry and a kind of music he can set to and make—that is, by keeping the law, by learning and obeying the rules which apply in each of the realms. But the goodness one thus makes is no better than the poetry produced by the same legalistic and mechanical means. One can be creative in the field of goodness by deliberate purpose and main strength as little as one can be thus creative anywhere else.

A. E. Housman, in his little book, *The Name and Nature of Poetry,* tells how his poems were written:

106

I would go out for a walk for two or three hours. As I went along, thinking of nothing in particular . . . there would flow into my mind, with sudden and unaccountable emotion, sometimes a line or two of verse, sometimes a whole stanza at once, accompanied, not preceded, by a vague notion of the poem which they were destined to form part of. . . . I happen to remember distinctly the genesis of the piece which stands last in my first volume. Two of the stanzas, I do not say which, came into my head, just as they are printed, while I was crossing the corner of Hampstead Heath between the Spaniard's Inn and the footpath to Temple Fortune. A third stanza came with a little coaxing after tea. One more was needed, but it did not come: I had to turn to and compose it myself, and that was a laborious business. I wrote it thirteen times, and it was more than a twelve-month before I got it right.[28]

I do not want to press the analogy too far; but the same kind of thing is obviously true in every phase of life, and not least in the moral sphere. Man's creative work never seems to him to be his own. The primary item in the Christian creed is: "I believe in God the Father Almighty, Maker of heaven and earth." God is the creator. We do not begin to know the meaning of that statement if we think of it as an affirmation about some remote and unimaginable past or about the universe in its formal totality. It is a statement about everything that lives and grows in nature or in the mind and heart of man. Creativity belongs to God and to God alone. We are at best instrumentalities of which this creativity makes use, the channels through which it

107

flows. True and living goodness cannot be built by the laying of one obedience upon another like bricks in a wall. It is rather like a tree planted by rivers of water which brings forth its fruit in its season. It is the working of grace; it is the gift of God.

This insight, I repeat, lies near the heart of Jesus' teaching; and because I have ventured to suggest earlier that Paul does not always see with his Master's eyes, perhaps it is appropriate for me to say again that here, at this most important point, he is a true disciple. He saw, probably the more clearly because of the failure of his own efforts under law (Rom. 7:7-11),[29] the inability of law to produce any kind of genuine goodness. Love, together with all its ethical fruits—humility, patience, kindness, faithfulness, gentleness, self-control, and the rest—cannot be achieved by our efforts or earned by our merit. What we need is the living Spirit whom we cannot summon, the living Fire which we cannot kindle but can only pray for as Elijah prayed for the fires at Carmel. The goodness of love is always and entirely God's gracious giving of himself to us—a gift which remains a gift even after it is given, so that for one to claim even possession of it, much less credit for it, is, in that same moment, to lose it.

Now in thus emphasizing the spontaneous character of the highest goodness we may seem to have opened the door wide indeed to the antinomianism which we set ourselves to refute. What happens to the authority and value of the ethical teaching if we decide not only that such goodness is never the result of our obedience, but also that it may in fact be bestowed on us as a gift of God? Is not the teaching thus thoroughly invalidated, and is not the role of the teacher reduced to irrelevance? The teaching, it would appear, becomes a mere description of a goodness for which we must rely only on God, and thus ceases to offer any dynamic challenge at all. It no longer lays on us any obligation. It does not tell us how a Christian *ought* to act—only how he *will* act. Indeed, since he is no longer under law but under grace, does it not become inaccurate to say that the Christian *ought* to act in *any* particular way? Such antinomianism may seem to follow inevitably from the recognition that the truest goodness is always and only the work of God.

Actually, however, it is not so. We have seen that God's action in forgiving us, far from invalidating the law of love as binding on us, presupposes our full recognition, in repentance, of its continuing validity and our acknowledgment and actual acceptance of the obligations it continues to impose. So God's gift of righteousness, free and undeserved as it is, presupposes the unremitting faithfulness of our devotion to his will, the seriousness and constancy of our moral effort. The recognition that the highest righteousness can never be the simple result of obedience to law, of the conscious and careful attempt to know and to do one's duty, does not mean that such an attempt is not required. It does not follow from the fact that the truest goodness is never the mere doing of one's duty that there is really no such thing as duty and therefore no point in one's trying to find it out and do it. It does not follow from the fact that the highest righteousness lies far beyond obedience that we are relieved of the obligation of obedience. In other words, I should say that Paul went too far in his reaction against a view which equated righteousness with the keeping of the law when he denied the continuing validity and the absolute indispensability of the law itself. In Jesus' teaching one does not sense any awareness that the recognition of law is in any degree incompatible with the recognition of the unlegalistic character of true goodness.

Nor are the two incompatible in our experience. If it is a manifest fact that creative achievement is never the product of effort, it is just as clearly true that such achievement never takes place apart from effort. One listens to the great performer on the violin or the piano and knows that here is something more than the mastery of an instrument; the musician has himself been mastered. One is witnessing not merely the performer's own skillfully executed effects, but the free creations of his genius. And yet, before this miracle of creativity could take place, an intricate technical discipline had to be acquired; and hours, days, and years of strenuous, self-denying work entered into the acquiring of it. Housman speaks of the effortless composition of his lyrics, but he lets us know also that the man to whom the poems so freely came was a literary workman willing and able to labor for months on a stanza and ready to produce and discard thirteen times. Again, I caution against pressing the analogy very far: creative moral goodness is not a work of art. But in this one respect at least the analogy holds: the true righteousness is not the product of man's effort and yet it cannot exist in the absence of effort. The righteousness we want we cannot make; but we must work at making it if we are to be in position ever to receive it. The gift of life cannot be bought; but only to those ready to spend all they have to possess it can it be given. So to the man who comes running, eagerly asking, "What must I do to inherit eternal life?" Jesus says in effect, "What have you *been* doing? Have you kept the commandments?" And he cannot answer the man's question till his own has been answered. Even then, his only immediate answer is the adding of yet another commandment, the setting of a new, and incomparably harder, task.

Knowing God is being known of him. Finding God is being found of him. But though by seeking we cannot find God, nevertheless it is those seeking him whom God finds. And seeking God is more than indulging in vague yearnings; it is giving up ourselves to his service and investing every power of heart and mind in the endeavor to walk before him in holiness and righteousness all our days.

Notes

[1] *The Christian Answer,* ed. H. P. Van Dusen (New York: Charles Scribner's Sons, 1945), pp. 161-62.

[2] I cannot hope to include in this book an adequate bibliography on the ethical teaching of Jesus or even to mention all the books which have been most helpful to me. The books I shall mention here come to my mind as important and have the added advantage of being readily available. Some of them are concerned entirely with the ethical teaching of Jesus or with some aspect of it. The others include significant discussions of the teaching or have important bearing, in one way or another, upon our understanding of it. I suggest: J. Bennett, *Social Salvation* (New York: Charles Scribner's Sons, 1935); B. H. Branscomb, *The Teachings of Jesus* (Nashville: Abingdon Press, 1931); R. Bultmann, *Jesus and the Word,* tr. L. P. Smith (New York: Charles Scribner's Sons, 1934), German ed., 1929; H. J. Cadbury, *What Manner of Man?* (New York: The Macmillan Company, 1947); C. J. Cadoux, *The Historical Mission of Jesus* (London: Lutterworth Press, 1941); E. C. Colwell, *An Approach to the Teaching of Jesus* (Nashville: Abingdon Press, 1947); M. Dibelius, *The Sermon on the Mount* (New York: Charles Scribner's Sons, 1940); M. Dibelius, *Jesus,* tr. C. B. Hedrick and F. C. Grant (Philadelphia: The Westminster Press, 1949), German ed., 1939; C. H. Dodd, *Gospel and Law* (New York: Columbia University Press, 1951); F. C. Grant, *The Gospel of the Kingdom* (New York: The Macmillan Company, 1940); T. W. Manson, *The Teaching of Jesus* (Cambridge: University Press, 1931); R. Niebuhr, *An Interpretation of Christian Ethics* (New York: Harper & Brothers, 1935); A. Schweitzer, *The Quest of the Historical Jesus* (New York: The Macmillan Company, 1950), German ed., 1906; E. F. Scott, *The Ethical Teaching of Jesus* (New York: The Macmillan Company, 1924); V. G.

Simkhovitch, *Toward the Understanding of Jesus* (New York: The Macmillan Company, 1924 and 1927); A. Wilder, *Eschatology and Ethics in the Teaching of Jesus* (New York: Harper & Brothers, 1939); H. Windisch, *The Meaning of the Sermon on the Mount*, tr. S. M. Gilmour (Philadelphia: The Westminster Press, 1949), German ed., 1929. Other pertinent and important books are referred to in other notes in this book.

[3] E. Stauffer in the article on *Agape* by G. Quell and E. Stauffer in *Bible Key Words*, Vol. No. 1 (tr. by J. R. Coates from G. Kittel, *Theologisches Wörterbuch zum Neuen Testament*), p. 47. Copyright 1951 by Harper & Brothers. Used by permission.

[4] Rom. 3:19. Paul is speaking presumably about man's state as confronted by the Jewish law, and when one considers how he interpreted the tenth commandment of the Decalogue (Rom. 7:7), one can understand his reaching this conclusion. Actually, however, he may well have been taking Jesus' life and teaching also into account—indeed, how could he have avoided doing so? Perhaps the apparent difference between Rom. 3:19-20 (cf. Rom. 7:23-24) and Phil. 3:6 is to be explained by the fact that in the latter passage Paul is recalling his situation under the Jewish law, whereas in the Romans passages he is speaking as one who has come to know the law of Christ. This is only a very tentative suggestion. And in any case (as will appear from our discussion in chaps. iv and v), I do not believe that Paul himself would have accepted any such explanation as sound.

[5] The question of how Jesus himself conceived of the relation of his teaching to the Jewish law, the Torah of Israel, is frequently discussed. He is reported (Matt. 5:17) to have said that he had come to "fulfill" the law. Does "fulfill" here mean displacing the law, or does it mean establishing or strengthening it, going beyond it but not beyond its real and ultimate intention? Undoubtedly Jesus' attitude toward Judaism and "the law" was understood differently in various parts of the church in the period when the Gospel tradition was taking form and, consequently, contradictory materials are to be found in the Gospels, especially in the Gospel of Matthew. I cannot believe that Jesus consciously repudiated the law by putting a new law in its place. It is more likely that he thought of himself as an interpreter of the essential meaning of the old law. On this issue see W. D. Davies, "Matthew 5, 17-18," in *Melanges Bibliques* (Paris: Bloud & Gay, no date given), pp. 428-56, and the literature cited there. So far as the argument of this book is concerned, the issue is, strictly speaking, irrelevant. Whether Jesus was establishing "the law" or displacing it, there can be no doubt that he thought of God as making all-important moral demands on us. These would have constituted God's "law" for Jesus, in whatever re-

lation he may have thought of it as standing to the traditional Torah.

[6] *The Journal of Religion*, XX, 88. Dr. Holt's words belong to a review of D. C. Macintosh's *Social Religion*.

[7] C. G. Montefiore, *The Synoptic Gospels* (London: Macmillan & Co., Limited, 1927) , II, 86. Used by permission of St. Martin's Press.

[8] J. Klausner, *Jesus of Nazareth* (New York: The Macmillan Company, 1925) , pp. 392 ff.

[9] *Atlantic Monthly*, November, 1930.

[10] Quell and Stauffer, *op. cit.*, pp. 28-29. Apart from quoted passages this summary is dependent upon this important article.

[11] *Ibid.*, p. 32.

[12] *Ibid.*, pp. 33-34.

[13] Montefiore, *op. cit.*, II, 80.

[14] C. H. Dodd, *Gospel and Law* (New York: Columbia University Press, 1951) , p. 42.

[15] Joseph Sittler, *The Structure of Christian Ethics* (Baton Rouge: Louisiana State University Press, 1958) , p. 50. Used by permission.

[16] "The Cry of the Age."

[17] Klausner, *op. cit.*, p. 396.

[18] See, e.g., St. John Thackeray, *The Relation of St. Paul to Contemporary Jewish Thought* (New York: 1900) ; W. D. Davies, *Paul and Rabbinic Judaism* (London: SPCK, 1948) .

[19] William Temple, "Christian Faith and the Common Life," from *Christian Faith and the Common Life* (London: George Allen & Unwin Ltd., 1938) , p. 53.

[20] I am aware that these paragraphs do not constitute an adequate discussion of the meaning of "justification" for Paul. Some supplementation is provided in chap. v, and I would ask the critical reader to withhold his final judgment upon my argument here until he will have read also what is said there about Paul's understanding of the relation of the believer to the law. On "justification" itself I have tried to state more fully the grounds for my own position in *The Interpreter's Bible*, IX, 393-95, 428-35, 450-52; and in *Chapters in a Life of Paul* (Nashville: Abingdon Press, 1950) ; pp. 141-57. On the subject in general one should consult Bauer-Arndt-Gingrich, *A Greek-English Lexicon of the New Testament* (Chicago: University of Chicago Press, 1957) and also G. Kittel, *Theologisches Wörterbuch zum Neuen Testament, ad. loc.;* (the article on this term and its cognates has been translated by J. R. Coates, *Bible Key Words* [New York: Harper & Brothers, 1951]) . Useful also will be the following: E. D. Burton, *The Epistle to*

the Galatians (New York: Charles Scribner's Sons, 1920), pp. 460-74; R. Bultmann, *Theology of the New Testament*, tr. K. Grobel (New York: Charles Scribner's Sons, 1951), I, 270-79; C. H. Dodd, *The Epistle to the Romans* (New York: Harper & Brothers, 1932), pp. 51-53; E. J. Goodspeed, *Problems of New Testament Translation* (Chicago: University of Chicago Press, 1945), pp. 143-46; A. C. McGiffert, *The Apostolic Age* (New York: Charles Scribner's Sons, 1925), pp. 140-47; Sanday and Headlam, *Epistle to the Romans* (New York: Charles Scribner's Sons, 1895), pp. 28-31; H. Lietzmann, *An die Römer* (1933). pp. 46-68; V. Taylor, *Forgiveness and Reconciliation* (London: Macmillan & Co., Ltd., 1941 and 1946), pp. 29-69. Also pertinent are Paul Achtemeier, "Righteousness in the New Testament," *Interpreter's Dictionary of the Bible* (to be published in 1961) and books on the ethics of Paul, notably that of M. S. Enslin (1930) and the unpublished dissertation of James T. Cleland (Library, Union Theological Seminary, New York).

[21] There are references in the Greek text of the story to "hired servants," to "servants," and to "slaves," but in the present connection the distinctions are irrelevant. All three terms stand in sharp contrast to "son."

[22] Quell and Stauffer, *op. cit.*, p. 61.

[23] *Ibid.*

[24] It is more usual now for commentators to regard this passage in Romans (7:7-25) as an ideal representation of some kind, bearing no close relation to the apostle's own experience. The issue does not lie near enough to the heart of the discussion of this book for any full consideration of it to be either necessary or appropriate, but it will be obvious that I tend to regard the whole passage 7:7-25 as being a personal statement. My reasons for doing so are briefly set forth in *The Interpreter's Bible*, IX, 498-500. I take vss. 14-25 to be an account of Paul's *present* experience under one of its aspects (an aspect, by the way, for which his *theory* of the Christian life makes no room) and vss. 7-11 as involving a reference to his earlier, "pre-Christian" experience. For other views of the meaning of the passage, see W. G. Kümmel, *Römer 7 und die Bekehrung des Paulus* (Leipzig: J. C. Hinrichs, 1929); A. Nygren, *Commentary on Romans*, tr. C. C. Rasmussen (Philadelphia: Muhlenberg Press, 1949), pp. 277-303; J. Munck, *Paul and the Salvation of Mankind*, tr. F. Clarke (London: SCM Press, 1959), pp. 11-13; and other literature cited in these books. The truth as regards this issue is not as clear to me as it once seemed, and the position I have taken is more than ordinarily subject to change. I should say, however, that even if Paul is not speaking specifically of his own experience, he is speaking of *human* experience and is doing

so on the basis of, and in terms of, his own. I do not see how we can avoid finding in this passage an important autobiographical reference—an authentic clue to Paul's inner struggles under the law.

[25] For another opinion on this point see R. Bultmann, *Theology of the New Testament*, tr. K. Grobel (New York: Charles Scribner's Sons, 1951), I, 341.

[26] A. Nygren, *op. cit.*, pp. 239 ff.

[27] It must not be overlooked that Paul did in fact not infrequently use the term "law" in other senses—to refer to what we might call an "order" or a "system" or a "constitutive principle," and also in references to the Torah in the most inclusive sense, that is, to mean the whole record of God's dealings with Israel, perhaps even the covenant itself. As an example of the first of these alternative senses, I would cite Rom. 8:2, and of the second, Rom. 3:31. In neither case is Paul affirming the continuing force of law *as command*. With only a little less assurance I should say the same thing of Gal. 6:2. But see the discussion of Paul's ethics in George F. Thomas, *Christian Ethics and Moral Philosophy* (New York: Charles Scribner's Sons, 1955), pp. 83-103. Also highly pertinent to the theme of the present book are pp. 17-82 and 105-141.

[28] A. E. Housman, *The Name and Nature of Poetry* (New York: Cambridge University Press, 1933), pp. 48-50. Used by permission.

[29] See note 24.

Index of Scripture References

Index of Names and Subjects

121